POWER TO THE CONSUMER

POWER TO THE CONSUMER

A History of Seeboard
from Nationalisation to Privatisation

KEITH MIDDLEMAS

Picture Acknowledgements

Most of the illustrations in this book come from
Seeboard's archives held at the Amberley Chalk Pits
Museum (particularly the pre-1970s subjects) and at
Head Office. The photograph on page 15 is
reproduced by permission of the Hulton Picture
Library.

ISBN 0 907383 38 6

First published 1993

© SEEBOARD plc
Grand Avenue
Hove
East Sussex BN3 2LS

Cover design by David Loftus

Printed and bound in Great Britain by
BAS Printers Limited, Over Wallop, Hampshire

Published by James & James (Publishers) Ltd
75 Carleton Road, London N7 0ET

□ Foreword □

South Eastern Electricity Board, which quickly became known as Seeboard, has occupied a very significant place in the life of the South East of England. Its history is a story of success as it grappled with the problems of postwar shortages, followed by rapid and sustained growth over a period of many years. It adjusted to the changing environment in which competition intensified and in which customers became more demanding of high standards of service.

In this book, Professor Middlemas has captured the essentials of each phase in the developing story, and succinctly outlined the contributions made by key personalities and staff in general. The success of Seeboard during this period laid the foundations for the creation and maintenance of a flourishing business in the private sector.

Keith Stuart

SIR KEITH STUART
CHAIRMAN, SEEBOARD plc

□ Preface □

This is the history of one Electricity Board, the South Eastern, in the years from nationalisation to privatisation. The story is told roughly according to a chronology, not of chairmen and managements, but of broad changes in the Board's commercial and social environment – in other words, through the interplay of managers, staff, consumers and wider national events. I have tried to show the context of an evolving industry as well as the local events, shifts in demand, leadership and innovations in corporate structure, and the underlying ethos of a public undertaking. The story is told from several perspectives, that of staff and workers, and consumers as well as management; at crisis points such as the 1953 floods, the 1973 oil crisis, and the hurricane of 1987; and with the intention of outlining some of the immense social changes which electricity suppliers both shaped and followed.

Inevitably, because of the records available, and the lapse of time and memory, the bulk of the narrative reflects the Seeboard central archives. Interviews with past and present members of the Board have helped enormously to give a sense of how it operated and how its ethos developed. But so also has the house magazine, *SeaBoard*, later *Seeboard News*. The cartoons may remind the reader that this company like others has its unofficial, irreverent side.

I am deeply grateful to all those who have helped me with their recollections or advice: to those now retired, Leslie Goodman, Douglas Green, John Fuller, Bob Peddie, Harold Pugh, Colonel Dell Rothschild, Tom Rutherford, John Wedgwood, and to George Squair, the recently retired Chairman; and to those still in post, to Jim Ellis, Chief Executive, Len Jones, Managing Director, Distribution, and Maunder Wide, Administration Director; and finally to Dr Peter Lambert and John Norris for their painstaking work in the archives.

K.M.

□ Contents □

*Street lighting maintenance from an electrically powered
vehicle in Brighton, early 1930s.*

□ Introduction □

Electricity has been the symbol of modernity for much of the twentieth century, as progress along iron rails was for the nineteenth. The founding fathers of giant electrical firms in the United States and Germany could agree on one thing at least: that freedom — defined as comfort and leisure for the masses — could only be achieved through use of this new source of energy. In 1901 the French novelist Emile Zola wrote, 'the day must come when electricity will be for everyone, as the waters of the rivers and the winds of heaven'.

The electricity industry in Britain began in the 1880s with a wave of speculative activity and over-optimism, driven by promoters and entrepreneurs who then found it hard to create a firm base among consumers. For a generation thereafter it lagged behind its competitors abroad. The very first undertaking, installed at Godalming in 1881, was one of several that proved uneconomic. One at Brighton was, however, commissioned in February 1882, and became the first to achieve long-term success. By 1887 Brighton provided a 24-hour service across 15 miles of bare copper overhead wire to supply 1,500 lamps.

Stimulated by the 1882 Act which regulated the industry, larger private companies invested in the supply industry, followed by municipal authorities whose undertakings predominated in the South East after 1900. Total sales in that year reached 152,000 kWh, but the gas industry still supplied by far the largest market. Britain had geared its industry and urban life early and most comprehensively to fossil fuel

Generating equipment at Brighton power station, 1887.

Design for Crompton street lighting installed at King's Road, Brighton in 1893.

and gas; electricity supply remained fragmented. In the 1900s, town and city authorities retained most of the infrastructure functions which we now associate with central government. At the time of nationalisation in 1948 over 600 separate undertakings still operated.

Improvements in technology and economies of scale however, associated with the names of Charles Parsons and Sebastian de Ferranti, ensured electricity's march into transport (suburban railways and trams) and industrial equipment. While Charles Merz's North-East coast network grew to be the largest single entity in Europe, in the south, the London, Brighton and South Coast Railway began electrification in 1909, the same year that de Ferranti promised to the Institution of Electrical Engineers that 'the future will be all electric'.

Unfortunately, most new undertakings remained small, turning out more direct current than alternating current to supply equipment of a great variety of standards. The boundaries between private and municipal undertakings hardened, encouraging local rivalry or complacent monopoly. Political dogma exploded, as Conservatives defended private enterprise, Liberals and Progressives the merits of municipal trading. London itself, city, metropolis, and centre of the Empire, remained fragmented in a spider's web of competing suppliers.

World War I provided a catalyst, once it became clear in 1915 that there was to be a long, hard struggle, accompanied by a huge demand for electricity for munitions production. Driven by the Ministry of Munitions and the Department of Electric Power Supplies'

The turbine room of Brighton 'A' Power Station, 1906.

requirements, companies built up larger generating and supply units and endowed these with the latest plant; 95 per cent of munitions factories came to rely on electric power. Sales leapt from 2,100,000 kWh to 4,000,000 kWh by 1918. But this was achieved more by enforced diversion from domestic users to industry, and by efficiency gains rather than extension. The basic lack of co-ordination and local rivalries remained, even when peacetime 'normality' returned.

Some planning had, of course, taken place. But the first sketch of a national organisation faded at the end of the war, undermined by political disputes. Lloyd George's post-war attempt to create a state-run infrastructure in the service of private industry was defeated when his Coalition government fell in 1922.

Four years later, however, while the youthful Labour Party dreamed of nationalisation, the Conservatives (led by Stanley Baldwin, a former ironmaster) reconsidered Lloyd George's state corporation. Spurred by the expert advice of the Scots engineer Lord Weir, whose indictment of the industry's inefficiency shattered public complacency, and Baldwin's sense of urgency in the face of German and American competition, Conservative Party objections were overcome. In 1926 they set up a state corporation – the Central Electricity Board – which was to create and run a national 'gridiron', by linking the best generating stations. On the other hand, the 600 undertakings were to buy CEB electricity and retain control of its distribution. As Baldwin put it, 'What we have in mind is a Board managed by practical men, closely in touch with the industry.'

The CEB worked well for twenty years, under the far-sighted chairmanship of Sir Andrew Duncan. The 132 kV national grid's first step connected London and the most densely populated and industrial areas of Britain by 1932. Bitter battles took place over selection of the main power stations, control of distribution and, at local level, wayleaves for the new lines; but an area scheme came into being in the South East as early as 1928.

Pylons, a shock to early environmentalists, became part of the landscape. Critics of modernity dubbed the 1930s' poets, Spender, Auden and MacNeice, 'pylon poets'; but the epithet signified progress rather than vandalism. By the mid-1930s, and at a cost of no more than £40 million, Britain's network had been made almost as efficient as that of the United States.

During the Depression, 1929–34, most expansion occurred in the relatively better-off South East and Midlands. By 1938, such was the consumer demand stimulated by the existence of a national grid that occasional shortages were being felt at peak hours – an ominous pointer to the future, and a comment on the essentially haphazard, market-led development in distribution and the service industry. But in

An early vision of the electric home, 1912, from Electricity for Everyone *by R. Borlase Matthews.*

A pylon photographed in the 1930s.

Croydon Corporation Electricity Department floats. Above: *Purley, mid-1920s.* Above right: *1930s.*

A poster produced by the Electrical Development Association, designed to increase and diversify domestic electricity use, c. 1923.

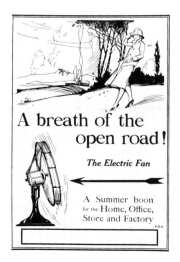

terms of costs, a virtuous circle developed throughout the 1930s: the more that sales increased, the lower fell the price per unit, from 5.75*d.* to 1.6*d.* between 1918 and 1938.

In the South East this benefited domestic consumers rather more than industry. Four main types of user now predominated. Suburban railways connected London to the bright new semi-rural suburbs (often called collectively 'Metroland') and rapidly expanding older towns such as Sevenoaks, Eastbourne, Hastings (in 1935), Maidstone and Gillingham (1939). By World War II, Southern Railway was carrying 370,000 commuters a day. Second came industry – not, in the South East, steel and engineering whose firms elsewhere often relied on private supplies, but docks (a crane could now be started at once, rather than after hours' delay to get up steam), new industrial estates, and small, even rural units such as dairies, quarries and sawmills. Thirdly, offices and shops, whose rapid growth paralleled the immense housing boom after 1934. Lighting, neon advertisements and traffic signs helped to increase commercial requirements ten times between 1921 and 1939. Finally, came domestic users: over three million houses were built in the decade, and household usage rose by an average of 17 per cent a year from 300 kW in 1921 to 5,000 kW in 1939.

The latter used only a quarter of generating output but brought in half the suppliers' revenue. From being a rich man's facility, electricity reached out to eight million houses, 65 per cent of the nation's stock by World War II. Hundreds of small electricians started up in (often one-man) businesses so that a 1930s house cost only £5 or £6 to wire, with far better bulbs and safer equipment than had been available in 1920. Standards rose all round, as did expectations: electricity was seen as a normal component of all new houses and offices, and local authorities came to accept that they should try to supply older houses also, usually on easy credit terms.

As electricity became affordable, the CEB, pressed often by local MPs in Sussex and Kent, encouraged additional rural supplies. More than 6,000 farms out of the total of 13,000 had been connected in the South East by 1947, a higher proportion than in the rest of Britain, despite the sparse rural population and wooded terrain, and despite complaints from urban users of being charged extra for these less profitable lines. The effect on the lives of farmers' wives was dramatic and was demonstrated in a film of the period 'The Village that Found Itself'.

An equipment revolution followed the change of public expectation, and flourished in the relatively affluent and leisured South East. New 10-amp sockets took a wide range of cookers, irons, kettles, water-heaters, fans and, above all, electric fires. The era dawned of Hotpoint and Hoover, Berry's 'Magicoal' fire with 'real' coals glowing in the grate. All saved labour, nothing more than the vacuum cleaner, half a million of which sold annually at £6 or £8. For the well-off, there were washing-machines, even electric carpets; for everyone in work the vision of the 'all-electric house'.

To tap this huge market, each undertaking opened its high street showroom, and soon found that wives rather than husbands came in to inspect, or ask about the cost, on newly available hire purchase. Advertisers aimed at a middle-class clientele, now hard put to find servants but appreciative of hygiene and good design, who discovered for themselves that the new equipment *did* save time. By the late 1930s higher-earning skilled workers in secure employment aspired to middle-class standards, in fulfilment of the promise articulated by the

An advertisement c. *1935.*

Eastbourne Corporation Electricity Department showroom, c. *1930.*

Bomb damage to Croydon Power Station during World War II.

Electrical Association for Women, that household chores might be cut by half from 50 to 25 hours a week.

After the barest minimum of emergency preparations during the 'phoney war', 1939–40, state control extended hugely in World War II. Early, misguided forecasts of a fall in demand were soon overtaken. The CEB managed to meet demand in all the essential industries at least until coal shortages developed after 1942. The grid and its stations in the South East survived the German bombing, though during the Battle of Britain 3 per cent of its capacity was sometimes put out of action. The worst moment came with a direct and totally disabling hit on Fulham power station; but occasionally barrage balloons drifted into overhead lines, and V1s and V2s caused severe damage in 1944–5. Building of new lines and the creation of a more efficient peak-load operation continued, but a serious backlog of routine maintenance developed.

Meanwhile, despite wartime restrictions on the use of electricity, domestic consumption grew steadily. The CEB's 1945 report forecast an extra 4,615 MW requirement by 1949, a proposal which, given the constraints of post-war full employment and competition for scarce materials and skilled workers, soon seemed impossible.

The political debate about state control, left over from the 1930s and only partly contained in wartime, burst out during the 1945 General Election and was apparently settled by the huge Labour victory. But although the electorate had voted, among much else, for nationalisation of basic industries, it was not clear that a change of ownership could remedy the physical problems arising from domestic demand, now freed

German prisoners of war, at the end of World War II, laying cable under supervision in Epsom, Surrey.

from all restraint after the harsh war years. One advertisement in 1946 caught the tone: 'Thank goodness Hotpoint are going to make life easier after the war.' Four hundred thousand new electricity connections were being made each year, sales of electric fires ran at a quarter of a million a month in 1946, and demand seemed likely to double every five rather than the predicted every ten years.

Electricity had, in fact, become too cheap, in real terms, and in comparison with coal and gas. But it took the terrible winter freeze of 1947, nowhere more severe than in the South East, to demonstrate how serious was the mismatch between supply and demand. Whatever Cabinet ministers had imagined in 1946, as they prepared nationalisation plans against a theoretical capacity of 11,300 MW, the CEB could deliver only 8,900 MW to meet a normal winter demand of 9,210 MW.

That winter was far from normal. The first wave of snow caused closures in the South East in the brickyards and cement works, and disrupted the emergency house-building programme. Then on 23 January 1947 the snow fell deep and froze for seven weeks, paralysing both the South East and the Midlands, making reality out of the Cabinet's nightmare 'Loss of essential production, widespread unemployment, no lighting or means of cooking, stoppage of trains and trams'.

One-fifth of all industrial workers were laid off in the South-East. All aspects of life suffered: transport, leisure, above all domestic and family existence. For those laid off, on a single man's basic rate of £1.10s. (against the average wage of £6.1s.), life ceased in any sense to be 'normal'; and it barely improved when cuts to industry were reintroduced in the first week of March, because the thaw was followed by floods of great severity, coastal storms, and exacerbated by sustained heavy rain. Full supply came back to households only in late April. Over the Seeboard area's 3,000 sq. miles, Kent and Surrey as well as East and part of West Sussex and a small part of Middlesex, millions found out what Hugh Dalton, Chancellor of the Exchequer, meant when he wrote in his diary 'the most satisfactory place these days is in bed'.

It was he added 'beyond a joke'. For the all-electric house (which now included a host of the new 'prefabs') it meant misery: potatoes put on the hotplate unboiled three hours later, frozen pipes, even greyhound racing prohibited. Deaths of the over-65s in Kent and Sussex rose during that time by 65 per cent. As the government discovered, consumers refused to put up with it; the state of emergency brought back too vividly memories of wartime conditions. Once it was over, the new nationalised boards were to be faced with the reality, not only of restructuring and investing to repair the six years' backlog, but of meeting consumer demand and satisfying consumer opinion.

A motorist looks for an alternative route on finding yet another impassable road near Sevenoaks in the big freeze of 1947.

□ CHAPTER □
1

Nationalisation

The model of a state corporation which should distribute energy through regional boards, each appointed by a Minister, had already been set out by Herbert Morrison before World War II and agreed by the Labour Party in 1934. In many respects, especially the balance between public-service duty and commercial principles, it resembled the old CEB. For that reason, nationalisation of the electricity industry aroused less opposition than that of the railways or gas companies, even among Conservative MPs like Brendan Bracken who harried Attlee's government unmercifully. The majority of managers, being conditioned to ideals of public service, would probably have agreed with the Electricity Supply Corporation's Chairman, who wrote in 1946, 'no one with any intricate knowledge of the industry can maintain that changes are not overdue, and could be brought in by any government in power'. Rather than fight, most private undertakings accepted their fate, and campaigned only for better compensation. Managers may have doubted whether the electoral promises of cheap energy, universally available, were feasible, but workers positively welcomed the change. Yet talk of worker participation, though fostered by the Left at the war's end, found little favour with the Labour Cabinet after 1945. The Electricity Act went no further than to enjoin the widest possible consultation between Board and employees.

Details of how the new central authority would operate took months to work out once the Act had been passed, and vesting date — on which all the municipal undertakings as well as private ones would disappear — was set for 1 April 1948. The implications could hardly have been exaggerated. As in the 1930s, electricity had already played a substantial part in Britain's post-war recovery. It started on vesting day with assets of £831m and plans for £650m expansion. The new British Electricity Authority (BEA) comprised the largest electrical utility in the Western world, one of the largest industrial units anywhere, and despite

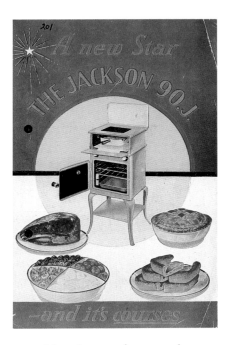

Advertisement for a popular electric cooker of the 1930s.

ELEKTRA—THE FAIRY GODMOTHER

Weald Electricity Supply Company promotional leaflet, c. 1935.

The Brighton Corporation Electricity Undertaking was one of the precursors to Seeboard. This poster appeared in 1936.

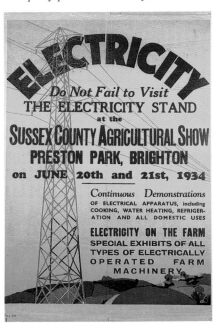

From early days agriculture has been recognised as an important market for electricity in the region.

Above: *At last, the beginning of the end of austerity. This Seeboard poster (c. 1950) announced the removal of the winter surcharge.*

Above right: *A reminder, from the early 1950s, of the days when solid fuel was normal in most homes.*

Right: *Typical Seeboard domestic appliance advertisement of the early 1950s.*

Seeboard's "Gifts with wings" scheme helps to give gifts that help

Electrical gifts are always welcome and if they help to save fuel they are doubly so.

Now Seeboard introduces specially for Christmas a "Gifts with Wings" idea which saves the bother of choosing, packing and posting and avoids the Christmas postal delays.

You simply buy at your nearest Seeboard showroom a gift card to the amount you wish to spend and send it to your friend. The card may then be exchanged for a gift which may be chosen at any of the Seeboard showrooms within the area shown on the map overleaf.

Illustrated here are a few examples, which you can see at your showroom, of the kind of gifts which are useful, fuel saving and can help to reduce the load on the power stations.

HERE IS A REPRODUCTION
OF THE SPECIAL
CHRISTMAS · GIFTS WITH WINGS ·
GREETINGS CARD

All prices include purchase tax where applicable

WARMING PAD. 50 watt. A little electricity gives much comfort. From £5.5.0.

PRESSURE COOKER. Speeds cooking, saves fuel. From £3.15.0.

READING LAMP. Eliminates use of high wattage central lighting. From £1.15.

ELECTRIC RAZOR. Saves hot water. From £3.10.0.

SMITH'S TIMER. Guards against waste of fuel and food. Price £1.4.6.

HAIR DRYER. 500 watts. Quicker than using a fire. From £3.12.6.

LAMPS. New lamps give more light than old. From 1/4½.

TOASTER. 600 watts. Uses less than a grill. Models from £2. Automatic £5.

FLEX HOLDER. Saves time, labour and electricity. Price 11/6.

GROUND BASE SAUCEPANS. Used with electric cookers — save electricity. From (Single) 15/6. (Set) £2.16.6.

recurrent constraints was to contribute 8 per cent of all UK capital formation until 1963.

The South Eastern Electricity Board was soon to be christened Seeboard and endowed with a coat of arms reflecting the chief elements of its area's heraldic history — an area which was and is heavily populated, despite large rural tracts and woodland. Roughly three million lived in its 3,000 sq. miles, nearly twice the density of the neighbouring Southern Board. Its scenic beauty, its coasts, and the long line of the South Downs required careful environmental treatment; ancient towns and villages were inhabited by the suburban middle-class who resented the arrival of too many overhead wires, while extensive built-up areas imposed extra costs. From the old regime Seeboard inherited fifty separate undertakings, seventeen frequencies and a fair proportion of customers receiving direct current. No obvious centre suggested itself as headquarters among the three principal contenders, Brighton, Tunbridge Wells and Maidstone.

Like other Area Boards, Seeboard's capital account was far in arrears, due to the backlog of maintenance and renewal that had built up since 1939. Endemic capacity shortages and lack of sought-after electrical goods deferred hopes of a quick return to pre-war service. The CEB had forecast that supply would fall short of demand by 1.5m kWh in 1948 and that the shortfall would not be met until 1951 — a date later postponed to 1954. A Ministerial regime of regulating or restricting demand therefore characterised the first five years, which inevitably fell mostly on households, entertainment, shops and offices.

Space heating bore the brunt, even though that was what domestic customers most wanted, as households switched from coal to electricity. The 1947 Budget brought a 66⅔ per cent purchase tax on electric fires and was followed by years of exhortation associated with Sir Stafford Cripps, cuts and low voltage, especially at the South Eastern peak hours 7–9 a.m. when houses were being warmed up in winter. Meanwhile the standardisation of tariffs, which all Boards brought in, raised some charges while lowering others. Domestic users found themselves additionally penalised by a surcharge, designed to reduce peak consumption in wintertime.

The new Board, therefore, had to operate in a difficult climate. It was prevented until the early 1950s from advertising for, or investing freely in, new business; and subjected to severe cutbacks in the next hard winter, in 1950–1. The 1947 great freeze had led the Attlee Cabinet to authorise a civil nuclear energy programme, and conditions of scarcity stimulated the drive to use more oil in power stations. But the first nuclear station, Calder Hall was begun only in 1953, and in the meantime the Boards had to struggle with things as they were.

Lord Citrine, first Chairman of the British Electricity Authority, c. 1948.

The beer tent at a staff sports and flower show, 1948.

The nationalised system is easily described. Like all the fourteen Regional Boards, Seeboard was given a three-tier structure: Main Board, sub-areas and districts. At the centre the British Electricity Authority (BEA), chaired by Lord Citrine, a former General Secretary of the TUC, took control of the power stations and the national grid, while the Minister himself appointed the Boards and set their salaries: £4,000 for Chairmen, half-way between a Minister and a Permanent Secretary.

Seeboard's first Chairman, Norman Elliott, had almost a free hand to find colleagues who shared his vision of a planned network, commercially run in order to achieve great economies of scale, but with a strong public-service orientation.

There could be no hope of an integrated power board, despite Elliott's trenchantly argued case for combining generation and distribution. The 1947 Act laid down that the BEA was to own the former; and despite problems over ownership, all the generating stations in the South East passed by 1949 to BEA's South East Division. This left the Board at the suppliers' mercy, for the bulk supply tariff (BST) was negotiated annually, invariably in an upward direction. Given that purchase of energy comprised 60 per cent of Seeboard's costs, while operating profits amounted to no more than 1.5–2 per cent of turnover, long-term budgeting remained problematic.

The actual transfer brought surprisingly few problems, partly because Elliott and his Deputy Chairman W. R. T. Skinner and the five Chief Officers had been appointed months in advance. By February 1948, these were already sending out questionnaires to discover exactly where they stood, who owned what, and how much plant and lines, how many offices, stores, showrooms, facilities and employees they were about to control. Wisely, Elliott persuaded some of the old undertakings who were grossly undercharging to bring their tariffs into line before the take-over, to defuse his future customers' complaints.

Some dispute occurred over whether to constitute four sub-areas or five. Surrey, centred on Dorking; Croydon and West Kent, on Croydon; Kent, on Rochester; and Mid-Sussex, on Brighton, already fulfilled the prevalent ideal of 'natural communities'. In the end, a fifth, East Sussex and South West Kent was added, largely to keep the balance of appointments. Since too many obvious centres offered themselves, Elliott chose the former Princes Hotel in Hove as headquarters – a fine late-Victorian building where in 1939 Neville Chamberlain and Admiral Darlan had met to discuss Anglo-French co-operation. After extensive renovation, during which the financial team sat at packing-cases instead of desks and the Board's surveyor broke his ankle in the dark in a hole left by the electricians, the Board was able to meet at last in February 1949.

Each sub-area resembled the main Board in microcosm, having a

The former Princes Hotel at Hove became the Board's new headquarters in 1949.

manager and four officers, and its manager received authority to make appointments in the medium salary range. District managers were given the same at lower scales. So much had been done by April 1948 that for most of the 9,000 staff, vesting day brought no more than a change of title and letterhead. Deep transformation took longer to instil. Secretary designate of Seeboard A. L. Burnell, then Clerk and Finance Officer of the London and Home Counties Joint Electricity Authority, recognised that it would be necessary to make financial arrangements for vesting day. The Act provided that the undertakings should pay into their banks all cash held at the close of business on 31 March and that these accounts would then be frozen. Arrangements had, therefore, to be made for each to have access to sufficient cash to pay wages.

Electricity showroom, Cranleigh High Street, 1948.

Arrangements were made for cheques to a predetermined amount and signed by one of two named individuals to be cashed at local banks. In the event all went well except in one small district, where the bank seemed unaware of the arrangement. Luckily the deputy manager stepped in and cashed a cheque on his own private account.

The next problem was the payment of creditors. Fortunately the JEA had a Central Accounts Office at Surbiton which included a large punched-card installation. This was used to pay the creditors of all the constituent undertakings from vesting day. To do this, stationery had to be specially designed. No one had a map of the future: as one engineer remarked, 'we walked a tightrope, blindfolded, for the first time'.

It was clear that the organisation, network, tariffs and style of

management had all to be wholly rationalised in line with the aims of efficiency and public responsibility. Some resistance was predictable, from municipal undertakings, sore at losing their identities, from consumers habituated to the old ways, from staff put under pressure or faced with a surge of customer complaints, and from the politically active in a predominantly Conservative region. The situation required tactful yet decisive leadership from Chairman, Deputy Chairman, and all five Chief Officers.

Norman Elliott, then 45 years old, came from the JEA, at the height of his powers, full of enthusiasm and panache. His excellent contacts in the industry, Whitehall and Westminster were to be of immense value during the next decade. His clear vision, authority and persuasive skills cut through the long meetings about integration which lasted through 1948. Evidently Hugh Gaitskell, the junior Minister under Shinwell, listened to his advice, for Elliott was able to bring with him from the JEA A. L. Burnell, as Secretary, and to choose W. R. T. Skinner as Deputy Chairman and C. F. Wells as Chief Commercial Officer from the Yorkshire Electric Power Company (somewhat surprisingly, since that had a reputation for opposing nationalisation). W. A. Gallon came from Woolwich to be Chief Engineer, and the highly capable Ernest Sinnott (whom Elliott called 'the whizz-kid of the industry') gave up his job as Worthing Borough Treasurer to be Chief Accountant. The solicitor W. H. Failes completed the team.

Having called it into being, Elliott let his team work in their own ways, reserving the big decisions and the style of management to himself and Burnell, and delegating day-to-day administration to Skinner and the others. However, he controlled co-ordination of the Chief Officers at the regular 'Coffee Party', of the sub-areas also every four months at the 'Tea Party', and the districts once a year at the 'Function': in all of which no minutes, only notes, were ever taken. It was idiosyncratic, yet it set the tone for years to come and helped to resolve Seeboard's basic dilemma — how to create a single identity out of fifty distinct rivalries.

Geographical necessity and the existence of 'natural communities' had created a structure which inevitably retained many pre-1947 boundaries. It was said, for example, of Rochester that a non-Kentish man needed a visa to go in. Regular lateral meetings between Chief Officers helped to resolve technical differences, but Elliott saw no way to harmonise the old identities except to blur them by central direction, until a new one should evolve. Hence the choice of new headquarters, defended despite criticism of its £160,000 cost; hence the technique of installing new, rather bureaucratic routines. All the same, sub-areas, mini-managements in their own right, perpetuated identities of their own. It took a long time at district level (and only with the help of the rolling programme of mergers to bring them into line with an ideal size of 20,000–25,000 consumers) before uniformity took root.

Elliott was not afraid to ask advice from outside consultants, nor to affirm that identity and loyalty should filter down from the top. The gains far offset losses of local pride, as functions and bulk purchasing were centralised, systems and transmission more rationally planned, billing, costing and accountancy standardised. Elliott determined always to cut costs and improve efficiency as a means to achieve the modest profit 'taking one year with another' which the 1947 Act required; thus giving his Board the best case to argue with the BEA for allocation of resources and for capital investment in the coming years.

Although Skinner conducted regular and valuable discussion meetings with 200 or more representatives of industry and commerce, Elliott took care of Seeboard's main external relations. These were, of course, regulated by the Act and the BEA. But much scope for informal bargaining existed, as Shinwell had implied in 1947 when he told the House of Commons that the BEA and Boards should keep in line on policy, but that London should not concern itself with local problems. Elliott got on very well with Citrine. In a climate where both BEA and Ministers preferred to negotiate privately rather than allow MPs or the press to intervene publicly, he was able in monthly meetings between Citrine and the fourteen chairmen to carve out rather more autonomy than some of the other Boards. Nevertheless his influence was fully stretched when it came to fighting for expansion. Even a modest deficit in a single year like 1951 required him to demonstrate just how far Seeboard had gone in achieving cost-efficiency and defining public service. It was with some exasperation that he wrote for Ministers' benefit in the 1949 Annual Report: 'our *customers* are our proper judges.'

Poster, summer 1949, lifting the ban on shop window and display lighting towards the end of ten years of austerity.

By Elliott's definition, managerial responsibility meant taking the fundamental decisions – albeit with consultation – so that Citrine's dream of industrial democracy, collective decisions almost Japanese in character, never materialised. It is doubtful whether after the first two years even Citrine believed in it. But Elliott's vision extended far beyond those first two years of reorganisation, to a strategic design of expansion within the margins set by government restraint.

There were to be no general increases of tariffs, only a continuous programme of economies of scale. By 1949, set tariffs had been established, either at a flat rate or on a two-part basis, with a quarterly charge and a lower price per unit. The average increase up to 1953 was kept under 6 per cent despite vastly greater rises in the cost of labour and materials. Seeboard was thus to operate on a narrow profit margin (only £423,000 in 1949–50 against a turnover of £17m). It would use the region's characteristics, such as the Sunday morning peak when

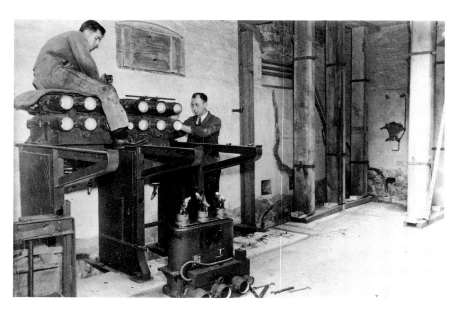

Fitters at work on Reyrolle switchgear, Croydon 1949.

housewives cooked the weekend lunch, to get a better deal on the Central Electricity Generating Board (CEGB)'s bulk tariff. It would go ahead with rural connections and if necessary educate farmers to use electrical machinery as well as lighting, through the use of lectures, exhibitions and Country Agricultural Committees. It would charge the full cost of these connections rather than subsidise them — but then, by applying the standard tariff, would subsidise rural customers indirectly without giving a handle to industry to complain. It would seek every way to increase usage in off-peak hours, for water and space-heating, and would chase up innovations such as the fluorescent lighting display installed in Eastbourne in 1949.

By October 1950, Elliott was in a position to outline a long-term plan: to increase consumers by 30,000 a year to what the Board judged to be a saturation point of 1.25 million by 1960. It was assumed that each customer's consumption would double in the decade (a lower rate than in 1945–8) and that the programme would cost £32m. In the circumstances of the cuts imposed to meet industrial demands consequent on the Korean War, this seemed ambitious, even audacious. Seeboard was in fact overstretched, mainly to supply new housing estates and to build the 11 kV line for Crawley New Town; and, having exceeded its allocation by 7 per cent, had to negotiate. It was the measure of Elliott's success that he got BEA approval both for the money and the plans.

Meanwhile the Chief Officers had their own problems. Burnell had to cope with the legal complexities of transferring fifty undertakings, their land and buildings, and negotiating over the generating plants.

(Ownership of one depot which had not generated for twenty years was disputed by the South-East Division of the BEA, but Elliott claimed it with the words 'I serve the State, you serve only the BEA'!) Odd anomalies crept out of the enquiries, including a small station at Faversham where the engineer, who ran a goldfish business on the side, kept his stock breeding in the cooling pond.

But the main problem for Burnell and Sinnott was always to discover where the Board stood financially. At first this meant simply the massive but routine task of getting the new bills out and keeping non-payment and theft of electricity to a minimum. In the longer term they had to evolve a comprehensive accounting system, ready for annual audit to the BEA, and here Sinnott demonstrated his flair, the fiscal eye of the Board, as Burnell was its legal eye.

An Agricultural Advice Bureau at Hayward's Heath Market, c. 1950.

Tariffs were based on a guideline that revenue should cover running costs. No concessions were made therefore to any interest groups such as farmers, nor to hospitals and charities. The two-step block tariff for domestic users varied according to a rough rule imposed by government to take account of the number of rooms in a house, which involved much argument over what constituted a room and some hostility, usually from among the better-off. But this did not mean real current cost accounting (which would have implied large increases for newer customers), only the costs of running a given supply on a historical basis. Before the era of high inflation, it served well enough – even between 1952 and 1957 the bulk-supply tariff only rose 10 per cent. Since tariffs for industry and commerce were tuned to annual rises in the BST, whereas domestic tariffs were not, the former actually subsidised the latter's peak demand.

In the engineering field, the problems consisted of extending supply to over 30,000 new customers a year, achieving compatibility between the newly merged systems, and ensuring standardisation and higher standards of safety and meter security. For several years mains reinforcements outweighed the cost of extensions. These central functions would always remain vital. But Seeboard staff also had to settle down, albeit at slightly higher numbers than before, 9,377 in 1949–50. Wages were to be bargained at national level, there being no other way acceptable to Citrine and the trade unions involved. Manual workers, skilled and unskilled, negotiated in London on the NJIC; the EPEA followed suit on the NJB, clerical and administrative staff on the NJC, a similar body, and senior management in the NJMC. Seeboard could therefore affect neither general wage and salary rates nor the impact of national strikes. The unofficial communist-inspired ETU strike in 1949 cut a fifth of generating capacity in the East and London. But Elliott took care to keep informal links open to local shop stewards, knowing that some access to the Secretary and his deputy would serve both as a safety-valve and as a way to ease some of the rigidity at national level. At Seeboard strikes hardly ever occurred.

Local level industrial relations centred on conditions of work, benefits, training and promotion. Seeboard entered the staff-training field very early on with a programme for an overhead-line school in West Kent. It also endorsed the National Apprentices Scheme both for craftsmen and students aiming at professional qualifications. Unfortunately, once qualified, the majority left for private industry, a sad comment on the general industrial attitude to training outside the state sector. Nevertheless, as Leslie Goodman, who had responsibility for industrial relations, noticed, many later returned, enticed by Seeboard's security and better conditions.

Tensions existed of course. The new jobs and duties assigned in 1948 involved stress; some staff were promoted but not others. In a wider sense also, expectations failed. Living standards in this industry had fallen relative to others in the post-war years and many skilled men were earning less, in real terms, than in 1939. These losses were not made good before 1959, which was not what had been expected of a state industry. Manual workers objected to clerical workers' more regular increases, and EPEA engineers worried about loss of the authority their skills had entitled them to, just as clerks were to do when mechanised accounting was introduced in the 1950s. Some workers lost privileges (though the Board backed away from cutting their concessions until compensatory measures were in place, and acted quickly on complaints that pre-war supplies of rubber boots and second-hand greatcoats to cable layers had ceased). Job security also meant less to a generation soon habituated to full employment.

The mood of the time blended hope for a great advance in public service, ably articulated in Norman Elliott's speeches, with nostalgia for the past, often displayed in the house magazine *SeaBoard*. On one hand Seeboard developed a sound collective spirit through its sports and leisure clubs, football and cricket teams, amateur dramatics and inter-club athletics. On the other, older employees hankered for the past. Hastings district actually talked of demoralisation among clerical staff who felt that their status had been downgraded. Some feared relocation, others less tangible things. For two years *SeaBoard* served as a lively forum, evoking a strong but carefully argued management response; then debate faded away, suggesting that the staff had settled down and that the new routines had eroded memories of an earlier golden age.

Too much had perhaps been expected in the very early days: that staff should act immediately as public servants, and ignore the inevitable jeers, either at them for being 'civil servants', or at the press stereotype that nationalisation was a recipe for waste and inefficiency. Seeboard

The first issue of SeaBoard *appeared in April 1948.*

replied robustly, spoke of its staff as 'ambassadors', but noted sadly that 'tariff alterations made it more difficult for consumers to like us'. In its publicity, Burnell often cited Elliott's 'private ambition, in a large scale organisation — which could so easily become a soulless corporation — to have a family spirit'.

Consumers were evidently demanding more from the supply industry than in the past. As the Board noted in February 1949, they expected 'the untrammelled use of electricity and appliances' and if not yet connected 'asked only how long they will have to wait and how they can speed up the process'. They carped at cuts, reduced voltages and the inability to supply fridges and cookers quickly; yet gave no thanks that the average tariff did not rise. Instead, as an *Evening Standard* headline put it, they seem to have subscribed to the view 'you own the electricity industry — AND UP GO THE PRICES'. Nearer home, Brighton and Hove Trades Council protested to the Board about 'the added burden on wage-earners and their families'. More factiously, the money Seeboard spent on its headquarters was subjected to two parliamentary questions by right-wing Tory MPs.

Gaitskell demolished both, wittily, and Seeboard responded vigorously, through the press. But it could not yet advertise for new business, not until 1951. Instead it emphasised its economies of scale, its plans for District Managers serving as many customers as lived in a small town to become their 'Mr Electricity'; and it made some imaginative gestures such as accepting liability for radios affected by changes of frequency. The Manager of Gravesend District even set out to address every annual meeting of the parish councils in his area. Seeboard targeted schools, interest groups like farmers, and the Electrical Association for Women. Later, when budgets eased, it began to support charities and other worthy local causes.

An Electricity Consumer Council had been set up in accordance with the 1947 Act, with representatives of local authorities, business and trade unions, heralding an era of formal consumer relations and a hope to implant Seeboard in a South East consciousness. At first it served more to funnel complaints to the Board than to explain Seeboard's constraints to the consumer; but at least the National Farmers' Union specifically exempted Seeboard from criticisms levelled at all the other Boards in 1951.

When had Seeboard fully developed an identity, as a region within a nationalised industry? The answer is probably 1951, the year when the total number of districts had been reduced to thirty-five from the fifty-five of 1948. Authority had been centralised as the best and quickest way to reach uniformity of practice and technology. But some powers had also been decentralised, to sub-areas and districts. As Elliott put it, Seeboard was beginning to achieve 'the initiative and flexibility of good small private businesses, wedded to the enterprise and wide horizons of great Public Corporations'.

□ CHAPTER □
2

Consolidation

Seeboard's pattern of leadership, its strategy and the limits of its autonomy within the structure of state industry were all set during the 1950s. In spite of the Conservative election victory in 1951, no concerted attempt to denationalise took place; but in response to back-bench MPs' feelings, the new Minister, Geoffrey Lloyd set up the Herbert Committee to review the supply industry's performance. Herbert's efficiency audit followed the 1947 Act's guidelines and largely vindicated the industry's management. But it also altered the context, by recommending that the CEGB's generating and transmission functions should be separated from the BEA, and that Boards should switch to current-cost accounting.

Westinghouse refrigerator, advertised in the early 1950s.

For the sake of equity between old and new consumers, all the Regional Boards objected to the latter and won their case. The subsequent 1957 Act indeed allowed them greater formal autonomy, making them responsible directly to the Minister of Fuel and Power. The BEA disappeared, to be replaced by a weighty though largely advisory Electricity Council. This gain was, however, offset by greater exposure to the bulk-supply tariff set by the CEGB, and in due course to the economic margins prescribed by Ministers.

Capital controls, high interest rates and hire-purchase restrictions persisted under the Conservatives, even after prohibitions on advertising for new business were lifted in 1953. Although demand surged exponentially once the great house-building programme began, the industry had to live with governmental stop–go macroeconomics as well as continuing high levels of purchase tax, not on cookers which were exempt, but from 50 to 100 per cent on all other electrical goods.

Meanwhile, the price of coal rose, erratically, but continually. Seeboard suffered worst, all through the 1950s and 1960s, being far from the coal-producing areas, by about an extra 3s. per ton, or 7 per cent compared with nearer Boards. Coal prices, Oil Fuel Tax (imposed to make deep mining financially viable) and the start of Britain's nuclear programme all fed higher costs into the bulk-supply tariff. On top of these external factors, Seeboard had to contend with nationally agreed wage rates, set without recourse to regional conditions, at a time of full employment and 3 per cent inflation. Trade unions in this industry set themselves to repair past losses by ratcheting up the basic rates.

In a region with a high proportion of domestic users, the option of raising tariffs at will was not in Seeboard's hands — even if it had wished to, or the government allowed it. Industry (28 per cent of consumption), commerce (16 per cent) and local authorities (3 per cent mainly for public lighting) were assessed according to each year's BST, but domestic consumers (53 per cent) were not. Financial reasons therefore compelled the Board to create a culture of economy, as Elliott warned in the 1951 report, and repeated after a particularly sharp increase in coal prices in 1955.

Shortfalls at peak times diminished after the early 1950s but Seeboard still had to contend with the less public, but more wearisome bargaining for capital allocations. In 1953–4 for example, having no alternative but to meet demand, Seeboard overshot by £156,000. In making this good, retrospectively, while cutting back on the following year, the BEA and ultimately the Minister induced a bad pattern of short-term thinking and tactical rather than strategic planning.

Seeboard's only way out of the prison was to cut costs, to make efficiency gains by standardising yet more lines and frequencies, and slowly to reduce staff numbers by natural wastage, from 9,300 in 1954 to 9,000 in 1958. Elliott was not afraid to call in outside consultants and

Seeboard advertisement, 1953.

Pioneer electrical engineer Dame Caroline Haslett, founder of the Electrical Association for Women, played an important part in promoting the use of electrical appliances in the home. She is shown here speaking at a civic occasion in the early 1950s.

Above: *Drovers Road rotary substation, Croydon, 1951.*

Above right: *Seeboard at the Purley show, 1953.*

Sir Norman Elliott, Chairman 1948–62.

the Board benefited greatly, in the clerical sector, from mechanised routine accounting and the introduction of electrical calculators. Lower down the scale, a Merit Prize scheme brought useful suggestions and savings, and in the 1957 *News Chronicle* competition, three of these reached the final printed list.

Conditions allowed Seeboard steadily to reduce its distribution costs per unit. Over the seven years to 1956, it fell by 0.164*d.* to 0.47*d.* – but with the perverse corollary that the bulk-supply tariff assumed an even larger share, 70 per cent of total costs. Until 1955, small and often unobtrusive tariff increases, amounting to 8 per cent since 1948, sufficed; but that year's coal price forced a 10 per cent jump from 1*d.* to 1.1*d.* Prices were pegged during 1956 but rose again by 9 per cent in January 1957.

Caught between consumer resistance and accounting requirements, the Board did well to maintain a satisfactory operating profit over the decade. But a loss followed the particularly severe bulk-supply tariff increase of 15.9 per cent in 1953. It was becoming clear that, despite steadily increasing demand, profits came not from selling power but from equipment, and from servicing and contract work – the pattern for a generation to come. Faced with a BST surcharge of £1m in 1957 and a resulting deficit of £807,000, it is hardly surprising that an ingrained resentment grew up, and a dream of one day achieving the right to generate Seeboard's own power and to set its own wages.

Short-term thinking ensued whenever plans had to be deferred, then revived, only to find they no longer fitted consumers' needs. Seeboard could rarely plan for potential demand, only what already existed. As a result the network always came first, often with hidden costs, when supposedly non-essential elements, like offices and depots, suffered. Elliott's informal approach allowed him to make gains in his own discreet way, but not to challenge the BEA's fiscal regime, other than by complaining in the annual reports that restriction was 'likely to cost the country dear'.

Nevertheless, Seeboard chose expansion even at the price of slower progress in standardising frequencies or converting DC to AC. Expansion of supply went without saying but sales and contract work required a broad measure of innovation and product development, allied to new showrooms, better sited to cover the region. The millionth consumer had been connected in 1952; connections thereafter rose by a near-constant 6 per cent a year, sales by 7 per cent a year. New lines averaged 550 miles a year, no longer so much to farmers (other than industrial units) but to new housing estates.

Facilitated by hire purchase, sales of appliances grew faster in the South East than in any other region save London in the 1950s. While the majority still cooked by gas, younger couples tended to use electricity. A quarter to a third of all households now had electric cookers or water-heaters or both, and benefited as coal prices forced up the cost of gas. Space-heating still consumed most units however and like all Boards save Eastern, Seeboard never fully costed this, even though later research showed that fires took half of peak load in return for only a third of domestic revenue. Almost endless expansion seemed in view, given that only one household in ten had a fridge in 1958, only one in five a washing-machine.

Seeboard took a lead in encouraging off-peak sales, at a rate set deliberately lower than some Boards, throughout the 1950s. Special lighting was provided for the Queen's coronation in 1953, the year that latticework road lighting first appeared on the A23 north of Brighton. Street lighting had become the rule by the mid-1950s, floodlighting for football grounds or Rochester and Guildford Cathedrals. The bulk of new sales came from storage heaters and under-floor heating in high-rise blocks of flats and offices. Supplies to industry now included fan

Below left: *The 'Hoover Spring Window', Merstham showroom, 1950.*

Below: *Coronation floodlighting, 1953.*

heating and air-conditioning and ranged from municipal spin-driers to water-pumping in the Ouse Valley. Above all, each of the 300,000 new houses built each year in the Macmillan housing drive could be supplied with a 13-amp ring main, with twelve light-points and four power points for £30.

Technical innovation brought, for example, steel-cored aluminium lines in place of highly expensive copper. Nothing came of talks with the gas industry about joint meter-reading at that time, nor yet of a visionary scheme for a two-way connection with the French grid; but from a small start in 1953 with a one-minute colour film, advertising extended rapidly. As late as 1956 the government still worried about peak-demand implications, but mobile showrooms, direct mail offers, and new forms of service carried the expansionist message. Thanet District ran a 'brides-to-be' course in 1956, Twickenham and Richmond another for 'modern brides', the assumption still being that only women did the cooking.

For many years to come the showroom would offer servicing as well as sales. Yet, echoing the old animus against 'municipal trading', politicians still complained about these 'luxury centres' unfair competition with private traders', and the image persisted strongly enough to deter Seeboard from cutting manufacturers' prices below the Resale Price Maintenance level despite its enormous bulk-purchase advantage. Fortunately this was not a decade of keen competition with gas, an industry increasingly crippled by high costs. Seeboard relied on the basic connection as the means then to open up what to 1950s' consumers appeared an endless revolution of expectations.

A decade of steady growth and cost-cutting was interrupted occasionally by the climate. Gale force winds and an exceptional tide brought immense floods in February 1953 to the Thames, the Medway and the whole North and East Kent coast as far as Dover. Faced with cables swinging and clashing above the flood-water, engineers had to switch off on a massive scale, then form commando-type teams to do the repairs. No lasting damage occurred to the system and as a result the Kent manager Harold Knell was awarded the MBE.

Lessons about small expert mobile teams were vindicated in high summer, on Sunday 29 July 1956, after violent thunderstorms had softened the ground. Gusts of 90 mph, worst of all in central Sussex, brought down trees, poles and conductors broadside. Short-staffed in the holiday, the engineers and linesmen needed a week to make good 12,000 separate breaks. In cases where trees were hanging, supported only by the line, they needed the skills and equipment of foresters as well as their own.

Seeboard's area was changing rapidly. The shopping centre with its novel frozen-food displays, the multi-storey office or block of flats

Showroom staff training course, 1956: 'How not to treat a customer, Lesson One'.

stand as 1950s images, like Crawley New Town itself. Quarterly bills ousted prepayment flat loading. By 1958 over half of all consumers had four power sockets. The phrase 'average household' was coming to mean one with a vacuum cleaner and a television set.

At the top, the original team remained with few changes. E. H. Skinner replaced C. F. Wells as Commercial Officer in 1953 and Sinnott was elected president of his professional institution while remaining Chief Accountant. Non-executive Board members retired in rotation, to be replaced by others, usually industrialists or directors of local standing. The first real breach came in 1958 when Burnell died, largely as the result of overwork. He had been a gifted exponent of Seeboard's public duties, reiterating always the message that the staff's work should be recognised, and the consumer seen as the ultimate judge. He was followed by George Wray, the longest serving of all Seeboard's Secretaries. Elliott himself maintained his links with the Electricity Council in London, as did the Chief Officers in their regular conferences. His obituary, in *The Times*, April 1992, pointed to his local reputation as a rugby referee – and hinted at the secret of his commercial acumen: 'there was a sneaking suspicion that he was not acquainted with all the laws, but the respect he commanded among the players overruled that problem.' Seeboard therefore remained relatively free from the feeling that 'the centre always dictated to the Boards'.

The essence of cost-cutting lay in raising Seeboard's staff's levels of skills. A slight fall in the rate of workers' accidents and a much higher decline in those attributable to negligence indicate an improvement in

Senior staff course, Hove 1957.

basic safety training. Informal management training, based on Harvard and MIT methods began, even though Seeboard was not able to afford a staff college until 1966. Residential courses met the needs of clerical and showroom staff, while engineering students went to Brighton Technical College on sandwich day-release programmes. Surprisingly, the trade unions showed less interest in industrial training than in wages at this time, and the issue of skills, like the level of manpower, remained matters for the Board's new standing committee on recruitment, training and education.

Because wages had fallen back relative to other industries and to the cost of living, the 1950s brought prolonged battles at national level in the NJIC, NJB and NJC. Much of this concerned differentials between manual and skilled workers. Only the results concerned an Area Board: but these were nearly all unpalatable, for rigid rules about grading and job demarcation gave Sub Area and District Managers endless problems, without local authority to settle them. Inevitably, restrictive practices grew up and spread widely, leading to lower productivity; equally inevitably, overtime increased, being the best, indeed the only means to increase take-home pay, often with management connivance but causing severe extra costs in the long term.

Given its slowly falling numbers and set policy of avoiding overtime whenever possible, Seeboard escaped the worst; but at the price of finding it hard to attract skilled workers from outside. This however had its own benefit, because instead local men could be trained and upgraded. Throughout, the margin between normal manning and the numbers required in an emergency remained narrow: close teamwork was therefore essential whenever flood, frost or gale struck.

*Seeboard's general commitment
to the welfare of the community
is demonstrated in this 1950s
road safety advertisement.*

*Seeboard poster (1952)
promoting the use of electricity
in the home.*

*But, as this mid-1950s
advertisement reminds us,
electricity supply was by no
means boundless in that decade.*

*To this day Seeboard has
promoted home cuisine in many
ways, in this case sponsorship of
a demonstration by the famous
television chef of the era.*

Above: *General domestic appliance advertisement of the early 1960s.*

Right: *The line graphics of this 1960 leaflet exemplify the style of the early part of this decade. Compare this with almost universal use of colour photography only a few years later (see page 38).*

Typical Seeboard shop of the 1960s.

ELECTRIC STORAGE RADIATORS
FOR WARMTH AND COMFORT IN SHOPS, OFFICES, DOCTORS' AND DENTISTS' WAITING ROOMS AND SURGERIES.

Get your heating at half cost

ASK HERE AND NOW

Better things are electric

By the end of the 1960s domestic central heating had become commonplace.

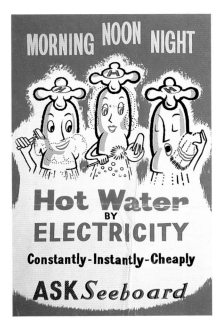

MORNING NOON NIGHT

Hot Water BY ELECTRICITY

Constantly - Instantly - Cheaply

ASK *Seeboard*

Water heating advertisement 1968.

NEVER MIND THE WEATHER
WITH SEEBOARD'S SPECIAL OFFER

FISHOLOW DE-LUXE ELECTRIC CLOTHES DRYER

GETS CLOTHES IRONING DRY AUTOMATICALLY

ONLY £37-16-0 or on easy payment terms
£3-16-6 deposit and 12 quarterly payments of £3-5-11. Total H.P. Price £43-7-6

Through the 1950s and 1960s Seeboard advertising reflected the rapidly increasing sophistication of domestic appliances.

Just fancy
electric water heating for only £14

an electric immersion heater will give you instant hot water in bathroom and kitchen

ASK *Seeboard*

Showroom poster 1960.

1968 Electric Refrigerators

See the attractive range

at your *Seeboard* **shop**

Better things are electric

We're converted–
we cook
electric!

Hot water on the spot

SEEBOARD
Water heater
£23·5·0
for kitchens & bathrooms

IMP
Water heater
£26·5·0
for offices, shops, cloakrooms

VANITY
Water heater
£27·14·0
for bedrooms & bathrooms

Prices include installation ready for use · easy payment terms available

better water heating is electric

By the late 1960s there was a notable – and permanent – shift to colour photography in advertising, made possible by improved reprographic technology.

On the leisure side, sports and societies flourished. Two Seeboard men had represented Britain in the 1948 Olympic Games, and the 1950s produced Bernard Robson, a well-known amateur lightweight boxer. In the ominous cold-war period, many Seeboard staff trained for civil defence, showing a level of awareness appropriate to skilled workers who would have been in key positions had disaster come. Meanwhile, reports from the Districts added an element of 'real life' to the Annual Report and John Boyle won for *SeaBoard* magazine its first award from the British Association of Industrial Editors.

Careful cosseting of the press began to elicit favourable receptions from local newspapers, notably for the 1956 Report, and for Burnell's talk 'Office Relations with Consumers'. Printed for wider circulation by the BEA, the latter was eventually translated into Tamil for the benefit of the South Madras Board! Nearer home, Seeboard was able to spend enough to hide some of the worst eyesores left over from the pre-1948 period; and good public relations work eased the Board's endless dilemma with environmentalists who protested about overhead lines, especially in conservation areas. Back in 1949 the Board had accepted a BEA guideline that the cost of burying lines underground was almost always too high: but it tried to respond, especially in historic town centres and villages, and by siting towers to fit the countryside's contours.

Apart from these protests, with their wide implications and press coverage, consumers' complaints reached the Board mainly through the Electricity Consultative Council. Commander Thompson and George Wray, the Chairman and the Board's Secretary, had established a consensual way of working, to such a degree that when the Herbert Report recommended separate offices, the Council at first refused, fearing to be cut off from Seeboard and its information. That it had no real power *vis-à-vis* the Electricity Council proved a recurrent annoyance, but it had few complaints about Seeboard's responses. Most consumer complaints were settled locally. Nearly all those judged to be justified concerned overcharging on small contracts, or poor voltage, which required line reinforcement. One gain made was that Seeboard abolished the rent on meters used for credit supplies; another that it gave free to 100,000 customers equipment on rental that was near the end of its useful life.

As Elliott put it, 'Electricity is not simply delivered at the door. It has to be taken right inside . . . it is an intimate, homely and personal business.' *SeaBoard* ran a series of pen-portraits of staff at the time, portraying the Accountant, the Display Man (at the Surbiton showroom — he said that 'good display can create the impression of a live business concern, while an inadequate one suggests a moribund, soulless and indifferent organisation'), the Maintenance Man and the Meter Man.

Advertisement aimed at industrial customers, 1958.

*Eastbourne pier
illuminations, 1949.*

The last two, out in the field, deserve mention. The first, typically replacing part of the Medway-crossing anchor structure, during a weekend, when after water-seepage in liquid blue clay 11 ft. down at 4 a.m. on Sunday, the workings collapsed. A new team started from scratch, shuttered it, pumped out, and finished after two dogged — but only 'routine' — days. The second, covering great distances by car to collect money in outlying districts, locating unnumbered cottages, fitted in with the seasonal workers of Kentish hop-fields or Sussex shepherds, and decoded messages like 'key under dustbin' or — for the trusted long-standing meter man — 'walk in'. A meter-reader of the period remembers trying to locate meters — five or more — on large farms in cowsheds or oasthouses and lofts. 'One often has to climb a few tons of coal, or bags of potatoes, to get near the meter, whilst another is in a shed a good half mile across the fields.'

Seeboard's first period ended about 1957, the close of the Citrine era. It had become true by then, even before the Herbert recommendations, that the Board was run 'as an economic concern . . . with a dash of missionary zeal. For besides running a great business, we believe we are also fulfilling a social purpose.' The Chairman's words were not the only test. The Board stood well with the new Electricity Council and its Chairman, Ronald Edwards, a former Professor of Industrial Organisation at the London School of Economics, for several measurable reasons. The post-war backlog had been eliminated: 4,000 miles of mains added to the original 14,764. The 33 kV system had tripled in size. Standard tariffs now applied to the great majority of houses, farms and the new category of churches and community halls. The operating cost per unit had fallen by 24 per cent in a decade. Less tangibly, an ideal of good service had begun to emerge not only from headquarters downwards but from the practice of District Managers, measurable by the low level of complaints.

□ CHAPTER □
3

The Long Boom

For fifteen years, until the boom broke in 1973, Seeboard was to live with the pleasant reality of steady sustained growth in consumer demand, for power itself, increasingly at favourable off-peak rates, and for appliances. Like its predecessor in the 1930s, the boom represented a broad social phenomenon, almost unaffected by the vagaries of government policy which ranged in these years from the 'dash for growth' launched in 1962 by Reginald Maudling to the Wilson government's National Plan. There followed the economic squeeze of 1966, public-sector deflation under Roy Jenkins as Chancellor, and finally the unrestrained, hectic spiral associated with Edward Heath and Anthony Barber, in 1971–3.

Seeboard advertisement, 1959.

Government actions did, of course, have an effect. But renewal of HP restrictions in 1960, or later credit restraint, even warnings not to advertise in 1966, never threatened a return to stop–go. Even when Seeboard rationalised its tariff upwards to meet the 1961 White Paper's five-year target of a 13 per cent return on investment, demand for power barely faltered, given the deep shift in public expectations. In the inter-war years, electricity supply to the home had ceased to be a rich man's whim and become a universal aspiration. The post-war era had fulfilled that, making it normal – even if some houses still lacked it. But even in the 1950s people regarded electricity in terms of basic lighting, cooking and heating, and were careful in their use both of a still-precious commodity, and the simple robust appliances they bought and used for many years, on HP from the very basic range available.

The 1960s brought revolutionary changes: the power to choose, at will from a wider range, on easier credit; and an assumption about novelty, new and better designs and regular technological improvements. That appliances would have a shorter, fashionable (if not necessarily usable) life turned into a positive advantage in an increasingly consumer-orientated society. Electricity was taken to be

41

Seeboard carnival float,
1960.

W. R. T. Skinner, Chairman
1962–3.

essential to house, office and industry, but was also taken for granted. Bedrooms would now be heated, not by coal fires but electricity in the new smokeless zones. 'Leaving the lights on' ceased to be a matter for recrimination.

Such changes paralleled those at work, where the employment of more women produced hundreds of thousands of two-earner households in the South East, and during leisure hours, for the house itself was becoming the focus of 'after work', with television, VHF radio, and hi-fi gramophones. Much of this fed into the designs drawn up by local authority as well as private architects. House plans now habitually included the full 13-amp ring main with square-pin plugs for half a dozen appliances. The business of new connections in itself ceased to be central to Seeboard planning, which was as well since the number fell from roughly 30,000 to 26,000 a year, to be replaced by considerations of supply, moulded by sales techniques and advertisements.

This profound qualitative change produced an easily measured quantitative result, above all in the areas of fastest housing growth and among higher-income groups. Wages in the 1960s regularly and predictably outstripped inflation. At the top end, in the 'stockbroker belt' from Sevenoaks to Guildford, emerged the heated swimming-pool, soon to be sited indoors and often surrounded by heated floors. But all levels of wage-earners reflected the pattern: skilled manual wage-rates rose 52 per cent from 1968 to 1973, and those of administrative grade 45 per cent, against a rise in the Retail Price Index of 35.5 per cent.

New devices fed consumption. In came the twin-tub washing-machine and the cooker with a timer, vital for working women. Cooker sales rose 17 per cent in the first year, placing electricity at last ahead of gas. Prices, especially of the expensive fridges, began to fall with mass production, ensuring that the Reigate District Manager's 'year of the happy housewife' (1960) would be perpetuated. Soon, to complement the shops' frozen-food displays, arrived the deep-freeze.

Meanwhile hire purchase was made easier, a development which sustained the whole boom, although cash sales also increased. So did teenage spending power, now that under-twenties could earn an adult's wage with few of the household or family burdens. Electricity had become relatively cheap again, as it had been in the 1940s: over the fifteen years, Seeboard reduced operating costs by 30 per cent, against 100 per cent rise in the cost of living – although that was not, of course, the case with the *price* of power, so heavily dependent on the bulk-supply tariff.

Starting with the 'whole home heating campaign' which was based on adding storage heaters one by one, Seeboard branched into under-floor systems, a favourite among local-authority architects. In 1966 however the 'Electricaire' system appeared, centrally generated on off-peak heat, but with fans and ducts to circulate the warm air throughout. It provided the first real electric central-heating, to rival earlier water-borne oil or coal systems and was soon widely used, for example in the 'ideal village' constructed at New Ash Green in West Kent and opened by Sir Keith Joseph in 1968. Seeboard's first heating centre opened that year in Brighton and drew the interest of architects, builders and developers. Later, in 1970 they tested the prototype of a wet central-heating – 'Centralec' – but with the resurgence of oil and gas, and cost inflation, its sales never matched 'Electricaire'.

In terms of units and appliances sold, the boom actually began in spring 1958, taking showroom sales to £4 million in one year. It grew largely as a result of the prolonged building of office blocks and towers of flats. Crawley's first stage had been completed, but a necklace of high-rise suburbs now sprang up in the GLC's area of South London, Kingston (the Tolworth Broadway scheme of twenty-two-storey tower blocks), Croydon (fourteen multi-storey blocks and 600,000 sq. ft. of new offices), Purley, and Beckenham. British Railways electrified their Kent line so that Seeboard was called on for twenty-six substations, supplies to signals and points, and 90 miles of 33 kV oil-filled cable in 1960–1. Suburban building for commuters followed all along the North Kent coast, marking a start to the developer's decade.

As in the 1930s, growth fed autonomously on itself. Sales to domestic consumers doubled to 1962 and doubled again, unaffected by tariffs or climate (17 per cent up in 1962–3, despite that terrible winter).

Advertisement, mid-1960s.

Seeboard's showrooms had to change, and did, not in numbers (for they stabilised around 85–90) but in their position in the districts, above all in their attention to better display and sales trading. In due course, super-showrooms emerged, such as the Crawley Centre, opened by Richard Wood, Minister of Power, in 1961. By utilising modern lighting and lay-out, and opening throughout Saturdays, they enhanced the attractions of Seeboard's own range of equipment.

Sales in 1966 showed a profit of £375,000 on a £7.8m turnover. Air-ducted central heating had taken off. A new scheme of credit sales with repayments made weekly or monthly over nine months offset the HP disadvantages of larger down-payments. Equally important, a second generation of products began to reach the shops, headed by transistor radios. The era of pop music, the Beatles and the Rolling Stones, heralded the arrival of the customer-selected hi-fi set and the Sony-Walkman. To beam the message at home, Seeboard used the commercial TV channel and BBC Radio Brighton, first of the new local stations, soon to be matched by Radio Thames and Radio Medway. The new theatres of the period, the Yvonne Arnaud at Guildford, and the Adeline Genée at East Grinstead, both installed electrical air-conditioning.

In 1970 each Seeboard customer spent on average £5 on appliances or equipment; £6 the next year; £7 in 1972. Increases of 15 per cent a year were soon seen to be unsustainable but it began to look as if the era of instant gratification had arrived. Seeboard's sturdy, medium-priced first range, comprising cookers, fridges, and water-heaters under the Elite label, had been superseded by the Seeboard brand of thirteen types in 1967. The early 1970s brought another improvement, the Electra with a range of twenty-three models, well designed, and competitive against private-sector showrooms. Seeboard had benefited from the abolition of resale price maintenance in 1964, not primarily by cutting prices, but by filling the mass-market slot, a share it held successfully, aided by sterling's devaluation in 1967, until German and Italian machines finally penetrated what had been a rather sheltered area.

To supply this market, Seeboard set up its central warehouse at Tunbridge Wells in 1970–1, stocked with the complete range, ready for rapid delivery by 26-ton freight-liner lorries. Linked to the main computer which was installed at Hove in 1967 and then transferred to Worthing, this brought great savings in costs, manpower and consumer tolerance. At its peak the warehouse could deliver 2,400 items a day.

Commercial sales techniques dominated every aspect. The 'White Meter', which provided cheap off-peak power for 9 hours a day, was hardly a technical innovation but it successfully demonstrated to a huge public the value of off-peak current. At headquarters in Hove, specialist salesmen now dealt with the specific problems of farmers or domestic users, light industry or office developers. 'Electricaire' was made central to a new concept of 'the integrated environment' and was displayed at the Whitgift Centre in Croydon, opened by the Duchess of Kent.

Given that competition with the gas industry stirred again, after years of placid coexistence (at least until coal prices forced gas on to the defensive again in 1972), sales professionalism had a certain urgency. 1972–3 proved to be the last good year, its £11.5m turnover due partly to a public rush to beat the introduction of VAT in April 1973 – imposed for the first time on cookers. Light years away from the homely methods of the 1950s, professionals trained at Seeboard's new staff college found themselves dealing with other professionals in local authorities and the private sector, with manufacturers, suppliers and designers as well as architects and developers. They had begun to shape and stimulate the market as well as serve its needs.

The Simon hydraulic platform was introduced in the early 1960s.

□ CHAPTER □
4

Seeboard's Political Economy: 1958–1967

The man who had done much to establish Seeboard's identity as a public undertaking with a sound commercial basis left it in March 1962 after fourteen years. Norman Elliott was appointed Chairman of the South of Scotland Board (which had the advantage of generating its own supply). W. R. T. Skinner succeeded him, but only for a year since he was already near retirement age, and Harold Pugh followed in 1963. But the Elliott ethos, idiosyncratic and outspoken, had already begun to alter, even in 1957, the last year when an Annual Report was prefaced by a characteristic homily about the need for consumer orientation. Seeboard no longer needed to make that case in front of the BEA and the Minister.

Pugh inherited a Board with 1.3 million customers, sales of 7,545 million units and a capital investment programme running at £10m a year. His was an odd choice of Ministerial appointment, since he was already 63 and had been Chairman of the larger Eastern Board. But Skinner had given the impression of being opposed to nationalisation and the Department of Energy, being convinced that Seeboard had gone its own way too long, had decided on a shake-up. The Minister was not then convinced that Sinnott, the obvious choice, had chairmanship potential. But apart from a three-year contract, and an impression that Seeboard needed reform, Pugh, like his predecessor, was given no instructions.

He decided that the Board had become too hierarchical, with too large a gap between Chairman and the areas and districts; secondly that many more professional training schemes were needed to raise the general level of staff skills. Not being an organisation man, and knowing that Sinnott would in due course reorder the three-tier pattern of authority, he concentrated on consultation, trading and personnel management. Seeboard's ethos was to approximate rather more to the spirit of the old Indian Army Corps of Engineers where he had served before the war.

Consultation did indeed become more frequent and the Board rather more open to suggestions from below as a result; also perhaps more humane, for example, in setting a cut-off point so that employees near retirement age should not find themselves out at night in a blizzard on Romney Marsh.

The climate in which Seeboard operated changed little under the new Electricity Council's regime after 1958. The Council turned out to be a collegial body, which relied on peer-group pressure to keep chairmen in line, and rarely took votes. It accepted the Area Boards' autonomy, and had no jurisdiction over the CEGB's freedom to set its bulk tariffs. Seeboard had no choice but to accept the latter. It remained subject also to Ministers' appointments and to controls on capital, since the EC merely channelled Treasury-approved advances. In 1958 the Treasury raised interest rates on loans and set a 60 per cent target of self-financing. Government retained indirect power and Seeboard had still to plead its case every year, on the basis of new customers connected, and systems modernised or repaired.

Seeboard was never free to spend but Pugh believed that even remoter rural areas — the only ones still unconnected — deserved supply as part of its public duty. Financially, it ended the 1950s with the best-ever surplus, £750,000 in 1959. But then the bulk tariff went up 9 per cent in July 1962, causing a deficit of £839,000. For a state industry in the years of stop—go, it was hard to adjust quickly and Boards were wrong-footed, for example by Selwyn Lloyd's freeze and pay pause, in the course of which all Chairmen were summoned peremptorily by the Electricity Council to justify past overshoots and current budgets. Peak demand still ran ahead of CEGB supply until 1963 and the shortfall made the severe winters of 1961–2 and 1962–3 much worse.

Below: *Cable laying, Surbiton, 1960s.*

Below left: *Mobile showroom, c. 1960.*

But the outcry which followed cuts over Christmas 1961, and the subsequent expansionist dash associated with Maudling and his 4 per cent annual growth target, soon produced Ministerial instructions to invest more heavily in the distribution system. Capital flowed more freely and the shortages of peak load faded away.

The government's 1961 White Paper, *Financial and Economic Obligations of Nationalised Industries* set out the criteria for change. Aimed rather more at the railways than the electricity industry, it nevertheless picked up earlier debates about cost-accounting and set a prescribed return on investment for the five years 1962–7. Although Seeboard had done well by Treasury standards, having achieved 59 per cent self-financing as early as 1959, it found itself saddled with a 13 per cent ROI (return on investment) requirement, or £12 million profit by 1967 – slightly higher than Southern at 12.4 per cent. Prices had to rise if investment were to continue.

Previous financial wisdom had been that prices were not elastic because of political constraints above and social constraints below. But in the long boom, it turned out differently: after the rise in prices, sales actually increased by 17 per cent. The public-service argument altered somewhat, since customers were seen to be willing and able to pay levels closer to true costs – albeit calculated on a historical basis. The 1967 White Paper, published by Wilson's government, added a test discount appraisal for all new plans, but otherwise vindicated Boards' performance.

With the new tariffs, sales of power at once resumed the larger share of profits. The year 1962–3 brought a surplus of £3.7m, the next year one of £4.6m, figures undreamed of in the past. As a result, Seeboard almost reached its target in 1966. Then came a BST rise of 9.2 per cent which cost it £3m and an overall 1966–7 loss of nearly £1m. The outturn for the five years was only 12.8 per cent. Seeboard had, in fact, reached the end of its economies of scale rather earlier, in about 1964, and entered a period of slowly rising operating costs, due partly to higher standards of safety, partly to the heavy load of extensions and reinforcements made necessary after the 1962–3 winter.

Lean years followed, the troubled times when the Labour government jettisoned its National Plan and imposed wages and price restraint. Tariffs had to rise 15 per cent after the 'severe restraint' ended in December 1967. But the fact that this was passed by the Minister, without a reference to the Prices and Incomes Board, showed that it was the inevitable consequence of outside causes. Though it affected consumer confidence for a time, the shock was absorbed in the long boom.

Wage inflation, however, could not be so easily absorbed. The trade-off between rates, earnings and overtime (take-home pay) continued despite the efforts of various government-appointed Councils or Boards to obtain negotiated wage restraint. Electricity workers, like those at Ford Motors, held a key position in the annual round and, like the car industry, trade union leaders were pushed from below by powerful shop stewards, and by union members avid to keep up in an inflationary decade. These managed to break the 1961 pay pause and as a result acquired a possibly unjustified reputation for creating inflation.

Managements' only counter lay in negotiating productivity agreements and loans. These started in 1963, the year when, after a work to rule, manual workers were reclassified as staff with annual salaries, instead of hourly rates, in order to secure manpower efficiency, new working patterns and less overtime. Such negotiations produced the only strike of the decade in Seeboard's area, at Crawley. The Board stood firm, despite pressure from the Electricity Council, and other Boards were duly grateful later.

Negotiations at each level and for each job took weeks of persuasion. There were no obvious sanctions, in this pleasant area of England, where good morale obtained, where Seeboard gave reasonable pensions and only slightly lower wage levels than neighbouring Boards enjoyed. Wastage remained low but recruitment relied on the region because already house prices and rents were acting as deterrents to newcomers from the West and North. Later, computerisation and the increased mobility required, caused problems and the wastage rate rose sharply among lower-paid clerical staff. The introduction of manpower budgeting, in particular, offended the increasingly autonomous sub-areas and districts but, though not ready to reorganise these out of existence, Pugh nevertheless insisted, declaring that 'the areas must not set themselves up against the centre'. Productivity schemes eventually included all grades up to senior staff, and in 1965 the overtime average dropped to 1.7 hours a week.

The greatest advance of these years occurred in training. Seeboard already offered a range of sixteen courses for foremen and charge-hands, technical staff and young engineers; a residential conference for District Managers; and a trainee scheme for meter readers and fixers, jointers and linesmen's mates. Pugh took special pride in founding the technical training centre at Whitfield near Dover. The need he saw was to raise the level of skills, but in a precise way suited to Seeboard's requirements for more limited specialisms and appliance-servicing than was offered by local technical colleges — closer in fact to what he had known in the Army's Corps of Engineers.

The college had full workshop facilities, welding-bays, blacksmiths shop, lecture halls and overhead-line training area, and it offered courses to both industrial and technical staff. Up to 200 apprentices, who all wore the same blue jean uniform, worked for their City and

Since Seeboard's earliest days agriculture has been an important market sector. This is one of a series of advertisements which appeared in the mid-1960s.

Guilds exam. Others went on as students to acquire professional engineering qualifications and managerial opportunity. These now tended to stay with Seeboard, as they had not done in the 1950s, enhancing corporate loyalty.

Seeboard lacked its own staff college until at last it was able to buy the fine late-Victorian mansion, North Frith from the Horne family. Once it had been adapted, in 1967, it offered lectures, seminar and demonstration rooms for management courses and the sales training that had already become essential to Seeboard's continued performance.

Meanwhile billing and accounting, and subsequently engineering planning, was computerised. The programme started with two Honeywell main frame computers in 1967. Training of systems analysts and programmers took place in-house during the five years which were needed for completion. This in the end included all headquarters and district personnel records and appliance stocking details. In the first year 150,000 accounts were transferred and the last areas put on in 1969. By the time the centre moved to Worthing in 1970, all calculations, including mathematical and statistical operational research into manpower organisation and methods, had been put on magnetic tape. The old skills were not wholly lost. One wage award came very close to the end of the financial year and involved much back-dating. Could it be done in time? This question was asked by the Deputy Chairman of the Southern Board, given the near impossibility of rewriting the program so quickly. 'Yes,' was the answer from Seeboard, 'we have a lot of elderly gentlemen with quill pens who can cope.'

Chairman, Ernest Sinnott (fourth from the left), and Board Members at North Frith, Seeboard's staff college, opened in 1967.

Mechanisation transformed operations in the field, bringing huge diggers, power-winches, rams and drillers for the line teams to use. VHF radio to headquarters made it easy to order spares or reinforcements, and a small number of mobile generators now kept current going during essential repairs. Lessons about techniques drew a sombre moral from the 1962–3 winter when, shortly after Christmas, frozen deep snow and ice downed lines across the whole region and made appalling difficulties for the repair teams, faced with iced-up switch gear. For six weeks it took hours to get to a substation, hours to do a simple job. But unlike 1947, despite 26 days load-shedding, little supply time was lost and consumers were able to keep warm at home even if they could not travel outside.

Technical improvements and the extended use of auto-reclosers meant that most faults on the 33 kV system could be kept down to two minutes (at Lewes when all three bus-bars were submerged in the floods of November 1960, the low-voltage feeder pillars nevertheless operated for three days without failure). PVC-covered cable became commonplace, alarm systems were installed to give early warning of faults. Fault reporting was itself computerised, with the perverse result that faults, many types of which had never been reported before, rose from 3,321 to 5,500 in a year. 'Live-line working' which required a high degree of skill, made the continuous process of line maintenance less onerous, since it reduced the number of interruptions to consumers. (Eleven teams using this technique were saving a third of a million consumer hours a year by 1974.)

In 1968 the last of the area control centres, covering Sussex, put a central system into operation, linked to the CEGB terminal at East Grinstead. Thereafter Seeboard headquarters had minute-by-minute information on the state of its entire network. By then DC customers, who had still numbered 6,000 in 1961, had all been given AC, bar one, a pleasure garden at Margate. Some 50,000 customers however still depended on non-standard voltages.

Such improvements removed many of the old sorts of customer complaints. But the Consultative Council had a higher profile and 1960s customers expected ever higher standards, an attitude vindicated by the House of Commons Select Committee Report 'Relations with the Public' (1968). Though no higher numbers were in the end justified, complaints did increase, especially after 1968, mainly due to misunderstandings about off-peak supply, or high-consumption objections when meters were misread or bills estimated from past records. In 1965 the Consultative Council noted 'some deterioration in the image of the industry, as seen by the general public, and unsympathetic comment in the press' – a phenomenon related to tariff increases, the government's imposed financial criteria, and the

One of a series of advertisements promoting the use of electricity in the home. This appeared in 1961.

This advertisement, 1966, was part of a vigorous campaign to promote electric central heating in the home.

A new outfit for sales demonstration staff, late 1960s.

H. V. Pugh, Chairman 1963–6.

perceived high cost of the CEGB's nuclear programme.

Seeboard showed itself sensitive to these perceptions. The Council's main effect was probably no more than to make the Chairman a good diplomat. But the South East Area had an unusual media pattern, being close to London; dependent on London television and newspapers, it had only one large-circulation local daily and two evening papers of its own. The rest, being weeklies, emphasised mainly local doings and therefore tended to probe into the details of what Seeboard did, rather than more general public-policy issues which the local radio stations picked up. Thus when it abandoned the old space element in the quarterly charge, in 1964, Seeboard brought in the new, uniform one in stages, in case the reform should seem to benefit the better-off living in larger houses. And it settled once and for all an old dispute about landlords overcharging on their own private meters, which the government and local authorities had avoided (fearing to have to enforce a maximum charge) by fixing its own: 0.25*d.* above the tariff.

During these years it had been possible to improve offices and Mid-Sussex at last got a proper headquarters at Haywards Heath. New faces on the Board replaced the last of Elliott's team, as Pugh retired in March 1966, to be replaced by Ernest Sinnott. Arthur Dent became Chief Accountant, Ian Mackay, another from the Yorkshire Board, Commercial Manager. Edwin Peel took over as Chief Engineer from the long-serving W. E. Gibbs; and Peel himself was also to serve for thirteen years. Archie Milne became Deputy Chairman in 1966 and the first woman, Miriam Joliffe, joined the Board from the Consultative Council. Another link with the past broke when government curtailed its civil defence programme: regrettably from the Board's point of view, given Seeboard's 'sound organisation and band of keen instructors' whose enthusiasm now had to find another outlet in the Ambulance Centre.

Seeboard still looked and felt a little parochial. It had few contacts with other Boards, other than its Chief Officers meeting others at the Electricity Council; nor sense of being part of a wider world, despite the Cross-Channel cable which now exchanged 160 MW current with Électricité de France. At a conference in Le Touquet, the Secretary noted how far behind the French were at selling appliances: they only sold electricity, yet their salaries and perks were much higher. (The 1957 reform had raised Board Chairmen's salaries to £6,000, but they fell relatively thereafter until the late 1960s.) This parochial, long-established and rather too rigid character Ernest Sinnott now set out to reorganise.

□ CHAPTER □
5

The Last Good Years: 1968–1974

Ernest Sinnott proposed Seeboard's second reorganisation to the Board in July 1968. The debate whether to modify the original three-tier structure had never wholly died out; but in Pugh's time it had revived, as headquarters became aware how the areas and even the districts had begun to behave as separate entities, each in their own fields. Knowing that there would be opposition, Sinnott took care to prepare the ground and to obtain advice from an outside firm of management consultants.

Their advice was to replace the existing horizontal links with a system of vertical line management stretching downwards from a chief executive; to redefine Seeboard's corporate aims more clearly; and at middle-management level to distinguish policy-making from executive work. The division would be enhanced by developing specialist centres,

Below left: *Exposed cabling across the flood-damaged Cannon Bridge, Tonbridge, 1968.*

Below: *A display in the ABC cinema, 1967. David McCallum of the* Man From Uncle, *a youthful Sean Connery, the film showing,* Bonnie and Clyde, *combine to evoke the period.*

Linesman making a compression connection.

new managerial techniques and computer-based control, on the lines of what was already coming into being at Worthing.

Without accepting the whole, the Board unanimously decided to abolish the five sub-areas and all the districts, and to institute fourteen new districts, each more closely under central control. These new districts would have a clearer commercial orientation and less of the former 'Mr Electricity' outlook. Within them, engineering, commercial sales and administration were separated as between financial and line management. Douglas Green and a ten-man study-group took on the duty of assigning boundaries, in the second half of 1968, and kept as close to the old ones as possible. Since responsibility for the 132 kV lines was to be devolved by the CEGB in 1969, the Board also set up three distinct engineering groups for Kent, Surrey and Sussex. The final plan centred districts on major towns, each with its less densely populated periphery, partly to economise on staff, partly to localise higher rural costs and to introduce an element of competition through emulation. But large variations remained in size, from 437 sq. miles (mid-Sussex) to 47 (Sutton) and in population from Croydon (145,000) to Tunbridge Wells (71,000).

It took courage and perseverance to see such a reorganisation through, in a concern twenty years old; and to do it from the centre, even though the project fitted contemporary British management practice. It was not envisaged that any managerial staff would be left out: all were to be invited to apply either for their own job or for one of the new posts at headquarters in Hove. But though the old area managers had had amiable relations with headquarters, given the light rein employed by all Chairmen, they naturally resented the loss of their own initiative. Prior to this, it had been possible to do the job almost without reference to headquarters, and many had issued directives as if they came from the areas not Hove. At first, Area Managers assumed that the process was cosmetic and some prepared lists of successful applicants, ready for when existing staff reapplied for their jobs, on the assumption that nothing would really change. In the event, a fair amount of transfer took place, local management teams were broken up, and members of staff transferred to Hove.

People adapted. The majority of Area Managers were already near retirement age. But one commented 'you're abolishing the wrong thing — in years to come, Seeboard will be five large units'. So in fact it became in the late 1980s, but in 1968 reorganisation in this form was correct, and came at the right time — indeed perhaps two or three years late. New linkages established themselves quickly, the more so since all policy matters and specialised functions had been transferred to the centre. The Board changed also: L. J. Simmons became Commercial Manager in 1970, Leonard Goacher, Chief Accountant in 1974 and Douglas Green Secretary, when George Wray died in 1972.

Throughout the 1960s and 1970s, there was a recognition that the

Seeboard district office, Portland Road, Hove 1983.

United Kingdom needed to be more competitive in an increasingly aggressive economic environment. Not only were international comparisons made but, within the UK, the process of inter-firm comparison was encouraged by organisations such as the CBI and the British Institute of Management. Area Electricity Boards had always compared notes and reviewed performance, whilst sharing freely ideas for improvements and cost-savings. Within Seeboard, the same process was applied by comparing the performance of Districts and formalising the exchange of information. The volume of management information that was produced increased significantly; and District Managers' and their sub-officers' meetings came to see the exchange of information as a means to improve results. It was not sufficient simply to be compared in a league table. Business plans were prepared for all departments and districts in which objectives were to be clearly stated and against which progress would be monitored. At District level, operating plan meetings normally lasted for half a day. The process was not perfect, but significant improvements in performance were achieved.

On its twenty-first anniversary in 1969, Seeboard celebrated a 7 per cent profit on a turnover of £100m. Ninety-two per cent of capital investment came out of retained profits. The Board was able to make a

Above: *Seeboard showroom, Guildford 1983.*

Right: *Seeboard showroom, Hove 1986.*

small tariff reduction in that year, but for the last time, because rapid inflation — the worst since the mid-sixteenth century — was about to begin. It was as well that the reorganisation had been assimilated and that the numbers of staff were falling, to 9,000 in 1969, 8,295 in 1973, consequent on the organisation and methods study, and the Chairman's incisive memorandum 'Organisation for the 1970s'. It was fortunate also that this reduction, achieved largely by natural wastage and a few well-cushioned redundancies, came at a time of full employment.

The chief way to achieve greater efficiency lay now through restructuring. Those responsible for industrial relations noted how effective the step-by-step process of negotiating productivity bargains had been in the late 1960s. Covering over 90 per cent of Seeboard's staff, they had gone further in electricity supply than in any other state industry, chiefly because national union leaders like Frank Chapple (ETU), John Lyons (EPEA) and the clerical and administrative workers in NALGO accepted the equation that high productivity equalled high wages, even at the price of fewer jobs. It is hard to make precise comparisons but Seeboard reckoned that it never paid less than the national norms and sometimes slightly more. Its redundancy payments, allowances to help staff move house, and policy to warn of change well in advance, certainly created a more co-operative climate than had been obtained in the 1950s.

The year 1970–1 brought a sudden sharp loss, the result of large increases in the price of coal and the bulk tariff, together with the national go-slow by members of the electricians' union in December. Being wholly constrained by external conditions, Seeboard reacted, necessarily with swingeing increases in the tariff: 5 per cent for large industrial and commercial firms, 15 per cent for small, 12 per cent for the two-part tariff and 20 per cent off-peak. These were scarcely mitigated by being billed in the new decimal currency. Quite simply, households and small businesses suffered badly.

A further loss of £3.9m clouded the following year. As part of the Heath government's attempt to negotiate tripartite restraint with unions and management, the CBI voluntarily offered a twelve-months price limit of 7 per cent, and all the Boards (who were then CBI members) had to accept, knowing what the implications would be. On top of such trading difficulties came the 1972 miners' strike which demonstrated for the first time since the War that coalminers had come back into the industrial wages arena, fiercely determined to restore long-lost differentials.

Seeboard returned to surplus in 1972–3 but only as a result of high sales, 13.4 per cent up on 1971–2. In the Annual Report, Sinnott warned that the coming year would be exceptionally bad; and the Board began to take a tougher line on bad debts. Lenient still in cases

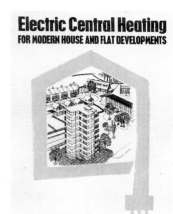

Promotional folder, 1969.

Live-line working at Rodmell, S.E. Sussex District, 1972.

Lifting a transformer at Seeboard's new central engineering store at Salfords 1973.

of hardship, it had given consumers credit for too long, as the Chief Accountant pointed out. The main cause of deficit up to this point however had been costs and wages – the latter especially since the Wilberforce Report (February 1971) had recommended a large wage increase for coalminers and special incentives to facilitate the next round of productivity agreements. Since the Electricity Council remained unwilling to face a national strike which could have threatened all the Boards' statutory obligations to supply power, wage inflation always ran ahead of the capacity to fund it.

Seeboard's ability to make medium-term plans ceased abruptly in 1972. Looking back on this time, Sinnott was to comment: 'In 26 years' existence, Seeboard has not experienced such a disturbing and crippling year.' The Heath government finally accepted that its long-sought tripartite pact on prices and wages could not be negotiated with employers and unions. In November it brought in the Counter Inflation Act: Stage I imposed an immediate freeze; Stage II provided a Pay Board and Price Commission, to start work in March 1973.

Like others, Seeboard had to submit its tariff increases to the Commission, whose criteria were of course affected by Treasury and DTI judgements about the effect on the cost of living index (RPI) and hence the impact on *future* wage claims, at a time when inflation had already reached 15 per cent. Domestic tariffs for 1973–4 were held therefore at 7.5 per cent, while industry and commerce found themselves exposed to the full effect on the bulk-supply tariff of a 60 per cent increase in the price of coal – even before they encountered the catastrophic implications of the OPEC oil shock in the autumn.

The year 1973–4 therefore produced the largest loss in Seeboard's history, £7.3m. The bulk-supply tariff had just gone up by 48 per cent. The effect was mitigated by a fuel surcharge concession made by the new Labour government, which allowed a 15 per cent addition to domestic tariffs. But this did not compensate for wages, transport or the knock-on effects of inflation on the sale of appliances. Whereas power sales fell by 1.4 per cent, appliance sales lost 9.9 per cent – a key turning-point in corporate fortunes. Neither did problems end there: 'threshold agreements', which had offered a way out for the Heath government back in summer 1972, were triggered inexorably by inflation throughout 1973–4, becoming in their own right a major cause of the upward spiral. When the Labour government introduced its Social Contract, the immediate effect was to secure in statutory terms powers of trade unions which, in a state-owned industry, were to make it extremely difficult to keep alive the sense of commercial practice in the years of recession and 'stagflation' down to 1982.

This is not to say that Seeboard's workforce was irresponsible, any more than national union leaders, trying to keep pace with the 16 per cent cost of living increases. Legislation came from above. Steering an energy industry through the mid-1970s crisis, when most policy instruments were controlled externally, would have involved rapid reactions which the existence of the Price Commission prohibited. Seeboard's task was however made worse by unfortunate accident. On an EC consultancy visit to Malawi, the Chairman contracted a severe illness which incapacitated him for much of 1972 and which recurred, so that Archie Milne, the Deputy Chairman and the Chief Officers had to carry an extra load.

Primed with responses to earlier bad weather, the Board's engineers and linesmen had coped adequately with storms and floods in September 1969. But the late blizzard of 4 March 1970 created 250,000 interruptions, the worst in Kent since 1947. 'Ice collars' brought a thousand miles of overhead line down and miners at Betteshanger Colliery were trapped underground until the engineers restored power to the winding-gear.

For the first time, Seeboard had to draft in gangs from neighbouring Boards and use Army helicopters: a lesson which led them to set up, with SWEB, South Wales and Midlands Boards, a special helicopter service for line maintenance and repair, based at Bristol. But these could not help when lightning struck the 132 kV grid in June 1973, blacking out Maidstone in probably the worst breakdown of the decade.

No natural disaster could compare with events on another stage. The national go-slow, 7–14 December 1970, brought controlled load-shedding — rapid switches of up to 5 per cent of Seeboard's customers

The Kent blizzards of March 1970: lines down near Betteshanger Colliery.

The miners' strike of 1972 led to power cuts. Here crowds gather around displays showing 'cutting rotas' in the windows of the Dorking Seeboard showrooms.

Ernest Sinnott, Chairman 1966–74.

— which at worst cut off 100,000 households. Despite special arrangements for hospitals, key factories and old people's homes, and notification via local radio and press, the public suffered severely and learned how dependent supply was on political factors. The long postal strike also disrupted billing and Seeboard's cash flow. Then came the February 1972 miners' strike, when NUM picketing caused a partial shut-down of coal-fired stations, and disconnections amounting at times to a fifth of all consumers. This time the Heath government issued directives, about how the cuts would fall, and although essential factories such as Beecham's plant at Worthing and the thirty-eight hospitals were kept going by special switching or mobile generators, many small businesses found themselves simply cut off for long periods as a result. One of the problems was that some firms tried to use their influence to bend the rules — something which Sinnott refused to allow. In such conditions, it was vital to tell people what to expect at every hour. The notification system worked well and subsequently the Board received large numbers of letters congratulating it on performance during the state of emergency. Even these troubles however scarcely compared with the 1973–4 winter.

The OPEC countries' quadrupling of the oil price in October 1973 left Britain with only eighty days' oil supply and precipitated a complex crisis of government. From Seeboard's point of view, the troubles began with an EPEA work to rule on 1 November, aimed to extract already-agreed payments from the ban imposed under Stage II. It worsened when the NUM started a thirteen-week prohibition on overtime, followed by a full-scale strike on 11 February. Having imposed a state of emergency on 31 December, the government passed an Order in Council, under which shops, offices and factories had to submit to a three-day working week.

Even after the election, restrictions of some kind lasted until 23 March 1974, forcing Seeboard to make routine rota cuts, interspersed with public announcements and advice to a public dismayed and disconcerted by the appearance of national breakdown. Television channels shut down at 10.30 p.m., voltage reductions continued throughout the winter, and sales fell sharply, since marketing advertising virtually stopped before Christmas.

Hove headquarters resembled a military command centre, with maps and schedules of the rota cuts, and an information room linked to all districts and showroom centres. Even in November there had been about 130 incidents a day where restoration of supply had been delayed, and the industrial relations climate was such that the Board could not rely, as in the past, on volunteers. Breakdown services only began to improve in January when the Pay Board settled the EPEA dispute.

Government-detailed rules gave Chief Officers much less freedom of

This photograph of high-voltage oil-filled cable drums gives a vivid demonstration of scale.

action than in previous emergencies, and over a longer period. But at least Seeboard itself was exempt from the three-day week, so that its staff could work at full speed throughout. Meanwhile, the Board had to impose a fuel-cost surcharge and a general tariff increase at the same moment, with the Consultative Council's agreement, to cope with the surge in the bulk-supply tariff. Short of structural steel, fuel and especially oil, the engineering staff had also to institute priority control over essential maintenance.

Once it was over, and Milne had expressed the Board's heartfelt thanks to its staff, some aspects such as sales returned to normal quite quickly. Looking back, *SeaBoard* compared the crisis to wartime, with streets blacked out and the public conditioned to 'grin and bear it'. But there was evidence of resentment, especially from shops and small traders, offset by the manifest efficiency of Seeboard's preparations and its relations with local authorities, police and emergency services. The installation of a new IBM computer in October, linking Hove, Worthing and the CEGB centre in London certainly helped.

March 1974, the month when Ernest Sinnott retired and Archie Milne took over, provided a point for taking stock. The centralising process had now been completed: engineering, accountancy, personnel records and commercial data had all been integrated on the IBM network. The existence of so much data, however, only emphasised that Seeboard's peak of market share had already passed in 1972. Ever-rising costs in the

Archie Milne, Seeboard Chairman, 1974–5.

bulk-supply tariff and government interference with commercial management would continue, as a Labour government with a narrow majority staggered into what had become a global recession. The gains in efficiency made painstakingly over twenty years had dissolved; since 1969 Seeboard's prices had risen only 57 per cent, its costs 118 per cent. An era of deficit trading and reliance on state subsidy seemed inevitable.

Meanwhile, the gas industry, empowered by the 1965 Gas Act to run both production and supply of gas, and freed increasingly from the price of coal by the arrival of natural gas first from abroad and then from the North Sea, stepped back into competition. Electricity demand itself faltered. Seeboard sold fewer units for the first time in 1973–4 as the boom in new offices and high-rise flats turned suddenly into a slump. Shackled to the increasingly costly nuclear programme through the BST, and to coal prices once Tony Benn the Energy Minister had drafted the 'Plan for Coal', electricity supply appeared doomed to decline.

Yet this was not Seeboard's impression. Sinnott, one of four Chairmen chosen to give evidence to the Commons Nationalised Industries Committee in 1972, thought that the Report more than vindicated Seeboard's record. Lord Penney, Rector of Imperial College and former Atomic Energy Authority Chairman, and Dame Elizabeth Ackroyd, a top civil service mandarin and director of the National Consumer Council, joined the Board. Such distinguished names would not have accepted nomination to a second-rate institution.

Dame Elizabeth began as she was to continue, heading the Consultative Council, by asking why only two women, Janet MacDonald and Barbara Wakefield, had so far attended the technical training centre. Soon she was to be the able exponent of a new sort of consumer relations, a formidable contender for the public-service side of Seeboard's life. Despite much clearing away of overhead lines in ancient villages like Steyning and Southease and along the Downs, which earned plaudits from Kent and Sussex County Councils, there had been an increase in public enquiries into proposed new lines. This reflected not only a changing climate of environmental thinking, but opposition from landowners to granting wayleaves, and most of all the sheer size of new 132 kV lines. The South-East was becoming a more discriminating and demanding area.

□ CHAPTER □
6

Nine Years' Hard Labour: 1974–1983

The electricity supply industry knew nothing but sustained growth during the long post-war boom. But the mid-1970s crisis developed into a double dip recession with only slight remission in 1977–9, so that underlying demand turned down, just at the moment when electricity encountered renewed competition from natural gas. This was partially mitigated by the rises in oil price in 1974 and again in 1980. But the industry's share of new national investment fell by 50 per cent in nine years. Worse, the second half of the recession brought not only a fall in sales of energy and appliances but a loss of roughly 17 per cent of Britain's manufacturing base, prolonged high interest rates and an overvalued currency, contingent on a monetarist policy, which combined to prolong deflation into 1983. That year, Seeboard's Annual Report plaintively expressed the hope for the *third* time in succession 'that the recession may be coming to an end'.

Jointer making a 'straight joint' on low-voltage cable, 1975.

As the trading terms changed, so did the political context in which state industries operated. Until now, Ministers and Chancellors of the Exchequer had used energy pricing as a tool of macroeconomic policy from time to time. After 1974 they did so continuously, and with more ideological intent to shape the economy as a whole. Until 1979 the Price Commission regulated tariffs; thereafter Margaret Thatcher's government imposed external financial limits (cash limits). Electricity had indeed been underpriced in 1974. By 1980 it cost in real terms 35 per cent more. But the bulk-supply tariff went up by that amount in just two years 1977–9, as a direct result of the long-term agreements which committed the CEGB to contracts for coal-burning power stations. Tony Benn's *Plan for Coal* proved to be another element to stimulate the Electricity Boards' dream eventually to escape from dependence on both coal supply and the CEGB's absolute freedom to set the bulk-supply tariff.

Denis Healey's anti-inflationary November 1974 budget envisaged a steady cut-back in government subsidies to state industries from £1,500m a year to £500m, the long-term consequence being to put the onus on consumers to pay. In the short term, it meant that capital spending was cut to the bone. Seeboard's 1974 corporate plan represented a complete reappraisal: line extensions almost ceased, maintenance was reduced, especially in costly rural areas, and staff numbers were to be pruned by speeding up computer work-programming and by substituting technical for human resources, for example through the use of remote-access terminals connected to computer headquarters.

The Board had no illusions about what price rises meant. According to the Commercial Manager Ron Gleadow, 'as the tariff begins to find its proper price level, it will encounter resistance in the market-place'. At first, caught between Price Commission control and 'temporary' compensation through tariff surcharges, Electricity Boards seemed unable to break out of the deficit-finance cycle. But in March 1975 government and Electricity Council agreed to start the way back to commercial operation by setting a 32 per cent increase for domestic users and a 10 per cent rise for industry and commerce. One result was to erode the differential between peak and off-peak charges so that it ceased to be possible again to offer the latter at anything near 'half price'.

A drop in the rate of annual wage increases from 15 per cent or more in 1974–5 to 4 per cent in 1976 facilitated a return to balanced budgets, at least until in October 1978 the TUC rejected a third year's pay policy. Meanwhile, urged on by the Council, Boards made some moves towards inflation accounting by adding a percentage for supplementary depreciation to historical costs. This pace altered abruptly after the Conservative victory, for the 'real costs' question raised by the Herbert Committee in 1955 recurred, supplemented by Treasury determination to reduce government subsidies to zero. Cash limits dictated that debt was to be repaid. Seeboard's share of the levy on the supply industry started at £9.8m in the first year and rose to £11.2m. Meanwhile true current-cost accounting converted 1979–80's small profit into a real loss of £17.9m. Since the Department of Energy required an ROI of 1.8 per cent on average net assets, the change had vast implications.

On the old system, Seeboard had made reasonable profits in the two years 1976–8 and had been on line for the department's earlier ROI target. It was now set back severely, not only by the new terms, but by cuts and deferments of capital projects like the planned new central engineering stores. Stocks were run down to the detriment of both

customers and suppliers, and credit to large users cut from twenty-eight to twenty-one days. These were only palliatives: the Board accepted that there could be no growth at least before 1982.

Losses continued: £7.4m in 1980–1, a year when even sales of appliances went into the red. Two tariff increases on quarterly bills in one year alone redressed the balance but inevitably hit sales and worsened electricity's competitiveness *vis-à-vis* gas. The economic regime continued, until at last in 1981–2 and 1982–3 Seeboard made an unqualified profit, achieved the ROI of 1.9 per cent *and* repaid £21.1m to the government via the Electricity Council. There was however a price. Sales of appliances had earlier, in 1975, been reduced by an increase in VAT to 25 per cent. Then they had recovered, particularly as new consumer goods, colour televisions, microwaves and easily fitted showers reached the showrooms. Even in the so-called 'winter of discontent', 1978–9, sales rose 21 per cent. Profits fell absolutely in 1980–1 not because the volume of business declined but because, in what had become outright rivalry with gas in the high street, Seeboard had to cut its profit margin to an unprecedented degree.

Since only 13 per cent of turnover was under Seeboard's control (the rest being the bulk supply) and since wages were the largest element, effective savings could only be made here. Staff numbers fell below 8,000 in 1976 to 7,647 in 1977 and stabilised for five years. Although shortages of electricians and linesmen persisted, the new remote technology allowed staff numbers to fall again after 1980, to 7,179.

The only other area of economy lay in cutting credit time on the domestic side, as had been done already for industry, commerce and local authorities. But to households paying a markedly higher tariff rate it was not enough to explain, as the Chairman and his Deputy did frequently, that for two decades energy had been too cheap. Efforts were made to distinguish between those who could but wouldn't pay

Above left: The opening of a nature trail in the grounds of the Seeboard staff college at North Frith by cricketer Colin Cowdrey, April 1978. Left to right: Robert Peddie (Chairman of Seeboard), Councillor Peter Adcock (Chairman of Tonbridge & Malling District), Tony Wilson (Conservation Officer). Geoff Rogers (Warden of North Frith) and Colin Cowdrey.

Above: Brighton 'B' power station, c. 1980.

Tom Rutherford, Seeboard Chairman, 1975–77.

Robert Peddie, Seeboard Chairman, 1977–83, enters the new council pool on Eastbourne seafront, 1981. Seeboard had installed energy-efficient electric heat pumps at the pool with a potential saving of 75 per cent over conventional boiler plants.

and the hard cases who could not. Seeboard devised special schemes for the elderly and households on low or fixed incomes (often in informal association with the social services); and 'Seecare', a way of saving money against the need for servicing or repairs. The Board's right to disconnect as part of debt collection became highly contentious, even when a code of practice had been agreed with the Electricity Council, and the then Chairman was loudly heckled at an Electricity Conference in Eastbourne in 1976.

All this was done under a rapidly changing leadership. Archie Milne, an astute engineer, served only one year, through the worst of the turmoil until March 1975. Though he set an example of tolerance and loyalty, the external conditions made it hard to do other than keep Seeboard on course. His successor, Tom Rutherford, represented a complete contrast, given his North American experience and direct northern style. He was able to compensate for staff losses, and the tensions that accompanied computerisation, by a novel informality apt at drawing the best out of the staff, together with firmness about high service standards and the absolute need to balance costs and revenue.

Popular and gregarious though Rutherford was, he also left after only two years, to manage the Northern Board, and his Deputy John Wedgwood, who had gone some way towards remedying the over-centralisation caused by reorganisation in 1968 by opening up new links with the districts (notably at monthly management lunch-time conferences) also left, to become Chairman of the Southern Board.

The new Chairman, Robert Peddie, came in 1977 from the CEGB with experience of the nuclear sector, having commissioned Bradwell, one of the early plants, and worked for the CEGB in the South-East. Having disagreed with the Minister about future planning, he was switched to an area which had not previously had Chairmen who concentrated so much on technological matters. At the time, Seeboard's external relations offered little scope for negotiation with Minister or Council: where necessary, the Board's part-time members like Dell Rothschild or Lord Penney usually acted as ambassadors. Long-term strategy also fell into abeyance, given the financial exigencies. Peddie therefore concentrated on technology and left his Deputy Chairman, first Len Goacher and then Bill Nicol, to deal with day-to-day affairs.

His assumption that the next cycle of reducing electricity supply costs would focus at the point of contact between supplier and customer led Peddie to think of giving every customer a terminal and meter with which (after some instruction) he or she could regulate household demand according to optimum cost. This was possible technically and in due course Seeboard put Calms (Credit and Load Management System) — whose unit (CALMU) was then a relatively large and expensive machine — on test, in the expectation that micro-electronic development in the 1980s would reduce both its size and cost. Unfortunately the experiment was later judged too costly and far ahead of its time. Consumers could not yet cope with what amounted to 'electronic mail order'. CALMU got support from the Electricity Council but none from the Department of Energy, despite its added potential for the gas and water supply industries, and Seeboard abandoned it.

Peddie's other experiment in using fibre-optic cable wound on the 33 kV line also failed, largely because it became unnecessary once British Telecom's communications services improved after privatisation. But he was successful in raising the interest of Seeboard's staff in computers, particularly among younger members, as the precursor both to quicker promotion and general upgrading of skills which the information technology revolution required. Though unpopular with more traditional members, and an outsider in the roll-call of Chairmen, Peddie committed what reserves were available to a cause which Seeboard's advanced position in high technology development later vindicated.

There was, however, some loss of direction and considerable turnover among senior officers. John Fuller had taken over as Commercial Manager in 1978. At the same time, the Chief Engineer, Edwin Peel also retired after thirteen years and Bill Kerss succeeded him. The Secretary, Douglas Green, retired in 1980, having been with Seeboard from the beginning and was followed briefly by Peter Humpherson and then in 1981 by Maunder Wide, who has held this office to the present day. Peter Humpherson, the former Eastbourne Chief Executive, went on to become Chief Accountant following the early death of Frank Barnes. These executives supervised the changes in Seeboard's organisational structure which made its financial management rather easier than the 1974 plan had envisaged.

Below left: A goodwill visit to the Tilmanstone Colliery 1978. After installing ventilation equipment on the surface, a group of Seeboard South Kent District men were given the opportunity to see the coal face. Here they are shown how to wear safety equipment.

Below: A team of Seeboard electricians carried out a £6,000 wiring scheme to light Canterbury Cathedral for the Queen's Silver Jubilee celebration.

*The Sheerness Steel Plant —
one of Seeboard's major
customers.*

*Seeboard laid power cables to
the only windmills in the
country to make a pair, 'Jack'
and 'Jill' at Clayton, near
Brighton, in 1978. Here three
of the cable layers are
pictured in front of 'Jack',
built in 1876.*

Steady-state maintenance was the most that could be achieved for the network, apart from new connections such as Beachy Head Lighthouse and the important 132 kV line to Sheerness Steel. Dover Port Authority had new requirements, as did the new smelting-plants, mainly for aluminium, which were set up in North Kent in the late 1970s. Capital allocation was rarely a problem in itself, once the case had been argued with the Electricity Council, but new works were still being submitted to intensive cost–benefit analysis. Rural amenity work continued, but sporadically, as in European Heritage Year 1975.

Computerisation became the central issue. All districts (now reduced to eleven) had received terminals by early 1976 and the interactive terminal system was completed in 1980. The telecontrol system, CADEC, developed by the Wiltshire Westinghouse Company, was installed over five years, 1978–83, together with three group-control centres whose VDUs gave sight of all fifty-one bulk-supply points and 235 primary substations. Seeboard's remarkable innovation was later replicated by others, but this did not diminish the significance of an innovation which allowed engineers now to spot faults and deal with most of them by remote control switches within 30 seconds. Half-hourly details of network load also covered the 33 kV substations. VDUs displayed stocks, so that showroom staff could by the early 1980s check availability at Tunbridge Wells warehouse and promise the buyer a firm delivery date while completing the credit sale.

Other new techniques included checking meter accuracy by a system of magnetic suspension (1976–7) and the introduction of microprocessors to automatic reclosers and the voltage-control system (1982). Meanwhile it became clear that the Hove headquarters needed drastic renovation. Hove Borough Council's original planning consent had been only temporary and they now refused to renew it; only to discover that no other tenant was willing to take on a Grade II listed Victorian building. By waiting, Seeboard lost the chance of a green-field site, yet in the information technology era it no longer mattered where headquarters was — so that when the Council gave way, a £6m refurbishment in 1979–81 gave the Board the fine and spacious offices which were to serve them well until the early 1990s.

Other opportunities for growth existed through efficient marketing, firstly of methods to save energy after the first oil crisis, and secondly to recapture advantage in competition with the Gas Corporation. Throughout the 1970s, Seeboard advocated better thermal insulation and efficient use of energy, in advertising campaigns and in the discussions held by its specialists with local authority or private firms, planners and architects. Some aspects such as heat pumps and dehumidifiers applied only to large buildings, and in general the public showed itself resistant to the idea of houses in which it was better not to open the windows for 'fresh air'. Nevertheless Medallion Homes, built to a design researched by the EC centre at Capenhurst, was sponsored in 1977. Six years later, nearly 1,000 had been completed. By then, new contracts were starting afresh after the long recession, with Wimpeys and Somerlee Holdings, and with McCarthy & Stone for small retirement homes and flats.

Over 2,000 executives from firms attended an 'Electricity for Industry' series of seminars in the districts in 1976. Wedgwood, the Deputy Chairman, represented Seeboard on the South-East Planning Council (a sort of regional Economic Development forum for the industrial community). Commercial Director, John Fuller mediated when large consumers complained, even though the answer usually lay with the CEGB and the bulk tariff; and through his audit team demonstrated that costs could often be cut by users themselves if, for example, they fitted time-switches.

New users of electricity added a little to sales. As millions turned to DIY – sometimes alas with fatal results – Seeboard found itself called on both for supplies and advice on safety precautions. But intense competition with the gas industry required reductions in profit margins and a wholly new sort of advertising. Seeboard joined London Southern and Eastern in the SELSE Consortium to advertise regularly on three television channels. Whereas it had previously been hard to find money to spend on showrooms, it was now able to programme improvements and resiting, and to tie them into the Tunbridge Wells central warehouse's bulk-buying. Contracting remained the Cinderella.

Staff reductions and changes in the pattern of work inevitably brought tensions. Technological redundancies mainly affected NALGO members who had reluctantly to abandon a rooted belief that size of numbers was the best measure of quality. More widely, however, Seeboard experienced erosion of the industrial worker and the rise of the technician. The 1960s' productivity deals had to be rewritten, thanks to data-processing of measured work and the management services unit's clearer picture of job specification and comparative-performance assessment.

Seeboard was not greatly affected by the Labour government's pay policies nor by the revolt of the low-paid in other industries during the 'winter of discontent', 1978–9. But for several years EPEA members defended both their skills and differentials against encroachment by industrial staff, particularly after the 1974 settlements which set grading patterns for the next six years. The industrial relations climate, however, improved after 1979, for both ETU and EPEA realised what the new government's policies implied, and distanced themselves from the TUC majority.

The hopeful tone of this period lay in the process of upgrading skills

"WHILE YOU ARE UP THERE YOUNG MAN, SEE IF YOU CAN SEE MY LITTLE DOGGY."

The winter of 1978/79 brought the worst conditions – wind, snow, flooding – for sixteen years.

A glider, its occupants and firemen had to wait for power to be switched off and the line made safe, before a rescue could be completed, when this incident occurred in South West Sussex District in April 1982.

Multi-trailer lorry for delivery
of electrical goods

throughout the undertaking and in evidence of collegiality. It was no longer merely through its sports and leisure clubs that staff related to Seeboard: 'staff' had ceased to mean industrial workers led by foremen, distinct from white-collar workers, and become a technical, clerical and managerial entity. Suggestions in the prize scheme, for example, now ran at over 1,000 a year, meriting awards totalling £3,000; which matched the total of all the other eleven Area Boards together in the early 1970s. Its original ethos, that consumers called the tune, survived the hard years. Dame Elizabeth Ackroyd, in the Consultative Council Chair for twelve years, proved an able exponent of any justified complaint, yet their number fell after 1976 to around 600–700 a year.

The Press Office could reasonably claim some credit for this, given its contacts maintained with journalists and local broadcasters as well as local MPs to discuss what were now seen as matters of common concern. This period witnessed a growing extension of Seeboard's charitable and sponsorship work. The year 1975 saw Seeboard's museum, named after the Chairman, Archie Milne, open in an old generating station at Tonbridge, with displays of equipment dating back to the 1880s; and publication of a short history of Seeboard's first twenty-five years.

A period of reaction and adaptation was ending. Seeboard had got through creditably and without much drama; and when George Squair arrived as Chairman from the Southern Board in June 1983, it seemed that the future would resemble the immediate past: tight budgets and no 'margin of comfort', to use the phrase of Jack Russell, a former Seeboard engineer.

□ CHAPTER □

7

◆——◆

Towards
Privatisation

The first signs of recovery after the three-year recession showed themselves soon after the new Chairman took office in 1983. For another five years it seemed as if the long boom had returned: domestic customers began to spend steadily on new sorts of appliances such as microwave ovens and cabinet fridge-freezers. A housing boom exploded, comparable in scale to that of the mid-1930s and as hectic as that of the early 1970s. Although competition with the gas industry flared up, demand appeared inexhaustible, being underpinned by two great social changes: first in the pattern of work, as shoppers turned to the 'new high street', Sainsbury's, Tesco's, and Asda's out-of-town stores for food for the freezer and microwave; secondly in leisure, as the home became the centre of electric entertainment with television, video, hi-fi and electronic games.

But the fences got higher each year on the financial side. Government targets for ROI on current-cost operating profit went up from 2 per cent in 1983–5 to 3.16 per cent in 1985–8. Seeboard surpassed both targets but was also faced with EFLs (external financing limits) debt repayment rising from £15.5m to £19.6m a year. At the time, the Treasury's intention was to make all state industries self-financing and free of government debt; hence the additional target of reducing 'real unit controllable costs' (i.e. salaries and materials) by 4¼ per cent by 1985 and a further 6 per cent by 1988. Seeboard achieved double these targets but at some cost to its operational structure.

The Board had to cut staff numbers; luckily the information technology revolution facilitated reductions from 6,892 in 1983 to just above 6,000 in the last year before privatisation. Increases in the tariff were judged impossible, given competition from gas. Tariffs, in fact,

As part of a national Electricity Supply Industry safety campaign Seeboard ran a poster competition in 1985. The junior section was won by Ruth Anderson whose father was a Seeboard engineer. The poster went on to win first prize in a national HESAC poster competition.

ran below the inflation rate for several years and were actually reduced twice after the oil price fall in 1986. Even during the long miners' strike, 1984–5, the huge extra costs of £66.9m were not passed on but written off against reserves; a less than satisfactory solution since it put off until 1990 the time when the Board would be free of the debt backlog.

Meanwhile, as part of the campaign to stir up state industries, the DTI referred the revenue-collection system to the Monopolies and Mergers Commission (MMC). Having selected Seeboard as one of its four test cases, the MMC took evidence during 1984–5. It noted diversity of practice and addressed most of its recommendations towards greater uniformity, including investment appraisal practice. On the public-interest criterion, Seeboard won a clean bill of health. On the more detailed suggestions for an audit committee, it was content to comply. It also scored a singular success with CALMU – as the Board noted 'a classic example where Seeboard initiative has been taken up nationally and field trials co-ordinated by the Electricity Council'.

Seeboard also came out well on performance criteria, less so on its percentage of bad debts, but average for its customer service. The MMC noted the presence of eighteen home economics advisers and staff visits made to customers at a rate of 50–90 a day. It is worth quoting the EC's own later performance records for 1987–8: Seeboard ranked sixth out of twelve Boards in its distribution costs but lowest of all in costs per customer, second best on staffing (numbers of employees per 1,000 customers), third on consumer service costs and second on costs of meter reading, billing and collection (see Appendix III).

This peak of efficiency had been reached by reorganisation as well as new billing and sales techniques and staffing cuts. Under Peddie, the fourteen districts had been reduced to ten. Six months after his appointment, George Squair introduced Seeboard's second major restructuring, aiming to reduce the rigidity and conformity to head office which seventeen years of centralised control had inculcated. In tune with management wisdom at the time, he intended to restore managerial responsibility to the point of service in the minimum number of self-sufficient areas, each capable of sustaining specialist services without constant reference to the centre. Four divisional general managers (DGMs) would run the second tier of line management and ensure a free upward-promotion flow.

As Sinnott had done, Squair brought in outside consultants, and set up an internal management group in 1985 led by Bill Nicol which initiated further change. Crawley, Croydon, Maidstone and Hove were to act as the divisional offices and the old districts were to be replaced by customer service offices. Authority for both training college and

staff college was to be held by the Warden at North Frith.

Monthly, in the Executive Meeting, the DGMs discussed their performance, as the Districts had done earlier and compared forecasts and budgets. Whereas in the past such exercises had sometimes felt like 'public humiliation', managers thought them now 'hard but effective'. As the implications of devolution sank in, they developed their own voices, and even challenged headquarters. It was not democracy but the transfer of appropriate responsibility: in European Community terms, true subsidiarity. Meanwhile, locally managed work units or mains teams, composed of managers and engineers at twenty-two strategic points, supplied the necessary flexible response to the needs of 1.8 million customers. These units, each of fifty to seventy staff with links to central IT services, obviated the need for over-reliance on computers from which some Boards later suffered, whose lower echelons could not always conform to externally generated requirements.

As in the 1960s, the impact of change on grades, terms and conditions required tactful consultation and negotiation with trade unions, and some compromises. Nicol's enquiry into manpower forecasting, for

Seeboard central warehouse, Tunbridge Wells. Container handling.

example, revealed that 20 per cent had previously been allowed for holidays and sickness. Change to bulk estimating – for meter reading – was not popular either with staff or customers but it was eventually accepted.

After thirty-eight years in the industry, the new Chairman showed himself an exemplar of 'hands on' management. He had a flair for detail and marketing, like Sinnott, yet like Norman Elliott also, a grasp of strategic trends. Seeboard's performance ratios indicated a vision of what was best for the customer, rather than conformity to an Electricity Council-inspired ideal. But to insiders Squair appeared to favour a prudent style, while to outsiders Seeboard (judged by privatisation criteria) came to be seen as somewhat conservative. He did insist on a culture of minimum expenditure, but as Len Jones who became Chief Engineer (later styled Operations Director) in 1984 also averred, 'a good engineer's profession is to manage costs as well as operations'. Seeboard staff, who had known him at Southern, accepted him as a colleague and came to share his intuitive understanding of how narrow the path to privatisation would be.

George Squair, Seeboard Chairman, 1983–92.

In the mid-1980s Seeboard had to steer carefully between economy and standards of consumer service. A MORI poll it had commissioned in November 1985, in response to the Electricity Council, confirmed that it gave more information to customers than most commercial organisations, but that there was a need both to improve standards and the Board's image. A lively debate followed, which explored how standard times could be set for responses, about how to improve the retailing activity, and how to explain the cost context of 'high bills' to aggrieved customers who saw only the quarterly account.

The result, the 'Seeboard 1987' campaign, drew on the experience of British Airways and the models of Marks & Spencer and Sainsbury's. Seeboard experimented with extended office hours, better control of van stocks for servicing and repairs, and improvements in staff/customer care. In 1988 it issued its Customer Charter (of which Jim Ellis, Commercial Director since 1986, was the architect), one of whose features was to be the £5 voucher, redress for failure to meet published targets. In the first four months this was to cost £6,700, usually in cases where a supply quotation had been misjudged, or of failures in the test-and-connect service, special meter reading and repairs and delivery. The numbers of complaints may have swelled because of the cash offer. But it exposed weaknesses and showed where the real complaints lay; and the Board later confidently raised the voucher to £10.

At the same time, Seeboard embarked on wholesale regrading of its seventy-seven shops. Managers found themselves with greater local responsibility, for containerised delivery from Tunbridge Wells, for a new type of service billing, and for initiatives such as installing dish-washing centres. Seeboard edged ahead in competition with gas once the government altered its rules to prevent the Gas Corporation selling North Sea gas 'too cheaply' (Seeboard attracted the allegiance of both Crawley and Worthing Councils who had been formerly devoted to gas). But budgetary consideration would not permit a price war with bulk superstores such as Comet, so Seeboard chose to go for good service, quality appliances, sold by well-qualified, often graduate staff, in ultra-modern shops, followed up with high-quality servicing. These sales staff now sold double-glazing insulation via sub-contractors, and showers — for Seeboard had bridged the old demarcation line between electricians and plumbers, just as the ETU had merged to become EETPU. DIY enthusiasts now received their spare parts by post.

By 1988, 16,500 Medallion Award homes and 5,000 Civic Shield homes had been completed. In the one growth area of the late 1980s, sheltered housing for the aged, Seeboard was busy in the London periphery and in retirement towns along the South Coast. After the savage cold spells of 1985 and 1986, and cases of hypothermia among the old, it launched 'Budget Warmth': a scheme to provide constant heat in one room for £3 per week, through the use of storage radiators controlled by computer-driven radio teleswitches. Eighteen local authorities signed on and nearly 3,000 such contracts were agreed. Good press and television coverage of 'Budget Warmth' was, however, offset by the problem of bad debts, already noted by the MMC. Related as this was to the high level of unemployment, particularly in East Kent, no easy answers suggested themselves.

The CADEC (computer-assisted distribution and engineering control) system neared completion. Other innovations included a second generation of computers in 1986, with 48 megabytes, 24 million instructions per second; high-security tokens to replace cash in prepayment meters; a colour videotext network; and in 1989 the first central-heating master-control system which at last allowed electricity to challenge gas on equal terms.

Consumers had long known that Seeboard was a competent supplier. But they now expected more. Commuters living in rural areas took for granted urban standards of service and security of supply. The auto-recloser had been in general use for some time. The future lay with automatic change-over switches on a ring main, attached to ever-shorter circuit feeders. In a very long-lasting network, change occurs slowly, usually only when units start to wear out. Now in its maturity, Seeboard had to face the long consequences of obsolescence and used the opportunity of planned replacement to meet a higher level of expectation.

The staff who serviced it all continued to train and upgrade their

Right: Since its early beginnings Seeboard has played an important role in agriculture and horticulture. Seeboard FarmElectric engineer, Stuart Higgins (right) with Mike Holmes of Neilsen's Plants in East Sussex, the winners of Seeboard's first FarmElectric Award for horticulture.

skills. Sixty to eighty apprentices a year took their City and Guilds at Dover, whilst Seeboard helped others through BTec and Open University courses. Under-24s embarked on Operation Raleigh and Seeboard sponsored sixty-five places a year on the Youth Training Scheme. To maturer employees it offered flexible leave to coincide with school holidays and career breaks to fit family or study needs. As an employer, however, it had also to use the chance offered by reorganisation to erode the old demarcation line between electrical engineers and industrial staff.

Once resolved, that issue was replaced by another, potentially as contentious, as Seeboard moved towards local pay-bargaining in the run up to privatisation. But changes in outlook in EETPU and EPEA, and rifts between them and the TUC in the climactic battles on another stage in 1984–5, facilitated compromise and a more co-operative climate. With larger industrial customers, relations had always been good and were cemented at regular meetings with executives from Seeboard's 180 major users during Industry Year 1986. Though a tiny minority of the 1.8 million customers, these used over 50 per cent of total supply: Gatwick Airport, Sheerness Steel, the Wiggins Teape Paper Mill, GKN Alloys, Sainsbury's, Brighton Marina, and the foundries, among them. The proportion increased when Seeboard won the contract to supply the tunnelling centre for the Channel Tunnel, the largest single traction supply in the UK.

Seeboard also maintained its contacts with schools, supported the Technical and Vocational Education Initiative, and gave 17-year-olds work experience. In the 1986 national competition 'The Energy

Facing page: Chargehand Peter Phillips explains to a local resident the processes by which Seeboard maintains electricity to remote rural areas. Linesman Ted Bravary carries out routine maintenance.

Linesman Alfred Knoefler working to replace a damaged insulator at Thanet during the 'little Siberian winter'.

The hurricane of October 1987 caused havoc throughout the region. Seeboard Chairman, George Squair, with junior Minister for Energy, Michael Spicer, surveying damage to high voltage lines brought down near Upper Beeding in Sussex.

Factor', its nominees, Gravesend Girls Grammar School and Worthing High School came third. Seeboard sponsored a popular cricket trophy for Sussex, Kent, Surrey and Hampshire; and performances such as an awe-inspiring rendering of Berlioz's *Grande Messe des Morts* at the Brighton Festival.

The South East had had its share of bad weather since 1947, but infrequently and briefly, so that until the storms early in 1987 Seeboard had never joined in the industry's insurance scheme. The 'little Siberian winter' which hit Kent for two weeks in January with heavy prolonged snow and icy winds changed its mind, and Seeboard joined in April. Line engineers had been cut off by drifts reaching 20 ft. on the Isle of Sheppey, and once again had used helicopters to keep the lines open to industry and to restore power to marooned villages. The RAF loaned others to carry transformers and the Army provided even a 17-ton tank. The worst problem had been the deposit of frozen, wind-driven salt on high-tension wire-conductors; at Thanet, the staff, including 64-year-old Alfred Knoefler, worked sixteen hours at a stretch through the night on a 100 ft. 132 kV line, in a wind of −10 °C.

Nothing however could have prepared them for the storm which hit the region on 16 October (the worst gale since the 'Great Storm' in 1706 sank shipping the length of the Channel and caused 8,000 deaths). Heavy rains had loosened the soil. At a time when trees in late autumn were still in full leaf, it hit a highly conserved region where for two generations forestry had given way to preservation, so that many splendid trees had in fact long passed their natural life.

A wind which gusted at Brighton up to 113 m.p.h. uprooted huge trees broadside, stripped their main branches, and broke outlying conifers in plantations half-way up, so that like giant flails they smashed whole acres beyond. Later aerial photographs taken by the Forestry Commission revealed that nearly 9 million trees had been lost. Deaths were few, unlike 1706, for it occurred between 2 a.m. and dawn; but the landscape, above all the famous gardens like Petworth, Leonardslee, Nymans, Wakehurst and Sheffield Park suffered devastation. Even in the parks and streets of London trees blocked the way.

More than 22,000 faults — the sum total of ten normal years — occurred, and 1.5 million out of 1.8 million customers (4 million people) lost their supply. While the 132 kV lines were high enough above the trees not to be badly damaged, 3,000 miles of the lower-voltage ones were put down and over 4,000 poles smashed. So vast was the disaster that, apart from restoring the 400 and 132 kV lines that same evening, Seeboard could not even estimate it. The 11 kV system had virtually ceased to exist. North Frith itself was cut off, sixty trees blocking the front drive, thirty at the rear. Reports of so many fractures jammed the Seeboard computer at East Grinstead. Massive obstacles confronted linesmen on the shortest journeys.

This Seeboard van was crushed by a fallen tree near Eastbourne during the hurricane.

Despite round-the-clock working, it was clear that Seeboard would need extra resources. Other Boards in England, Scotland, Wales and Ireland contributed, in all, 3,144 extra staff and supplied cables and poles from their own stores. BICC worked through the weekends to keep up cable production, and the Army provided a Commando team and Gurkhas to help cut ways through on the ground. By 19 October all urban areas had been restored, leaving 100,000 customers still cut off on the 11 kV rural lines, in the densely wooded central area from Guildford to Ashford, and along the whole northern edge of the South Downs.

All the incomers, even from Scotland, were staggered by the devastation. Two of them, linesmen, died before the work was finished. But by 31 October, after two weeks, they had all gone. Seeboard's men could cope with reconnecting the remaining 20,000 homes. Throughout, they had organised public meetings, information points and media notices. Much of the repair work was, of course, temporary: on occasions, linesmen had used half-fallen trees as substitute poles. Full, permanent restoration and replacement was to take another twelve months.

Seeboard lost £1.2m income and had to pay the direct labour costs of the extra staff, but mercifully insurance covered the bulk of clearance and repair. Its cover of £30m for any one disaster had to be shared with the Eastern Board which caught the gale's tail-end, but Seeboard in the end had to bear only a £600,000 excess. For the Emergency Review

Below: *Peter Statham (right), Seeboard's site engineer for the Channel Tunnel project, discussing preparations for laying cable on the 14 km route to the Folkestone site. Seeboard installed the network for the electricity supply for the UK side of the Channel Tunnel, for the running of trains and the operation of the terminal.*

Right: *Jointer Max Peters completes the replacement of a section of high-voltage underground cable.*

Panel, led by David Lovesey the Deputy Chairman, it was a test case of Seeboard's capability, in which the Board and its staff coped remarkably well. The team effort and the sense of purpose shared with the incoming engineers and linesmen from all parts of Britain found full expression not only in their report, but in Seeboard's 'Hurricane Specials' and in letters of congratulation from customers and MPs alike – and (more significantly) in the personal interest shown by Cecil Parkinson, the Secretary of State for Energy.

It is fair to conclude that the plaudits were not hyperbole. Although there was no precedent, there were no major errors: the only lessons concerned more use of underground cable and of bundled line, enclosing four cables in one for greater strength, which were both practical and environmentally sound.

Back in 1975, the Plowden Committee had recommended that the electricity supply industry should be centralised on the model already adopted for gas. But the then Labour governments were preoccupied with more urgent matters and the Boards vigorously contested even their modest 1978 White Paper. After 1979, the Conservative Minister David Howell, on Treasury advice, concentrated on the issue in terms of making the industry commercially profitable and reducing its dependency on state subsidies. Balked at achieving parity with Sir Denis

Superstore, Purley Way, Croydon, opened 1992.

Rooke and the Gas Corporation, the Electricity Council's Chairman Sir Francis Tombs resigned in 1981 and was replaced by Sir Austin Bunch. For another seven years, commercial self-financing remained the ostensible aim, even though the 1983 Energy Act allowed a small amount of generation outside the CEGB monopoly. Despite talk of an infusion of private capital, Treasury rules barred the way, and the Nationalised Industries' Chairmen's Group managed to deflect a 1984 proposal to treat Boards' assets as share capital on which dividends ought to be paid to the government.

Privatisation slipped on to the agenda in a modest way in 1984–5, partly as a New Right solution to a 40-year-old problem, partly as a means to raise money to reduce the Public Sector Borrowing Requirement – partly also to reduce the powers of public-sector workers. The latter consideration barely applied to electricity supply, which came late in the day, after the successful launches of British Telecom (1984), British Gas (1986), British Airways (1987) and British Steel (1988). But there were signs which Board members could read, and they made responses, such as changing part-time members' style to that of Non-Executive Director, and setting aside £13.5m after a 1986 discussion about the need for a corporate communications network. They also decided to produce a more dynamic annual report 'worthy of a large company' with a 10,000 print-run.

From the Chairman, the period required a carefully judged steer between becoming a profitable state industry providing the cheapest service – as British Airways did before 1987 under Lord King – and shaping Seeboard as a concern which could be privatised in its own right, rather than forming a mere adjunct of an all-industry launch like British Gas. Though the latter idea seemed to have been buried, it recurred in the guise of 'large regions', each grouping three or more Boards, but effectively still under Electricity Council control.

The Conservative election manifesto for the 1987 election made it clear that privatisation would come, but not how. The new ROI target however for 1987–8 required increases in tariffs of 25 per cent, staged over three years, which were, Squair told the Board in January 1988, 'needed to make the industry an attractive proposition'. His problem was to ensure firstly Seeboard's autonomy, and secondly that the drive towards privatisation should not trap Seeboard in short-term City-based calculations about flotation to the detriment of long-term development.

While the reorganisation and operations groups under Jim Ellis and Len Jones prepared the way in detail, the Board considered how to present itself – an enquiry into its outward image and inward identity which called even the name Seeboard into question. Meanwhile its Chairman took a large but informal part in the battle for the Minister's

Drafting the Seeboard prospectus, November 1990: Maunder Wide, Administration Director, standing fourth from left.

ear over whether the Area Boards should be privatised singly or the industry split into larger lumps. By then the Prime Minister herself had turned against both the Gas example and the privatised monopolies like British Telecom. Squair had strong cards when he argued that Seeboard would lose its regional identity and stored-up loyalties. There were real differences amongst Boards in their financial and cultural as well as physical aspects which could not easily be assimilated. Moreover the 1987 hurricane had deeply impressed the Minister with evidence of Seeboard's self-reliance.

Privately the twelve Chairmen, meeting in Harrogate in February 1988, gave Cecil Parkinson guarantees that they could and would ensure their Boards would be made ready for flotation separately. But they had little influence on the generating sector and did not question the government's long-held assumption that nuclear power was both the fuel of the future and cheap. When the White Paper appeared, followed by the Bill in December, they welcomed it vigorously, demonstrating loyalty to their guarantee.

Seeboard encountered little opposition among its own senior staff but had to convince many trade union members that the old ideals of customer service were not to be abandoned. Competition would in any case mean changes in job security, work conditions and the closure of some retail outlets. One whole issue of *Seeboard News* (March 1988)

Above: *Seeboard ran a series of posters as a charitable enterprise to help raise revenue for local hospitals.*

Above right: *In 1990 Seeboard carried out a major reinforcement to meet the energy demands of UK Paper PLC's vast new papermaking machine at Sittingbourne. On the machine, George Squair then Seeboard Chairman (right) and UK Paper's Chief Executive Monty August.*

took up the questions, welcoming the clarity of responsibilities to come to shareholders, to the new regulator, Professor Stephen Littlechild, head of OFFER, and to the consumer. Something of a crisis of identity did occur, nevertheless, and the Board found it wise to draw up a corporate identity manual and to adopt a new slogan, 'Seeboard – Doing a Power of Good'.

Seeboard reached vesting day, 31 March 1990, with a fair profit margin of £27.2m, thanks to the first stage of the three-year tariff increase, on a turnover close to £1,000m. But with the onset of recession, sales became stagnant, housing starts were falling, and unemployment rising steadily in the South East; these conditions were to obtain for at least another three years.

Under privatisation, Seeboard was required to separate distribution from supply and to allow no cross-subsidies. It would buy power from whoever offered it (mostly National Power or PowerGen) via the National Grid Company's network; and it would negotiate through the pooling and settlement agreement – in effect on a spot market, ruled by daily quotations and monthly settlements. It would have some monopoly characteristics but would open its network to challenges by others for the largest consumers and would itself issue challenges out of its area as a 'second-tier' competitor. Distribution charges were still to be regulated by the Secretary of State according to a cost-of-living formula and Seeboard was obliged to make all new connections without discrimination and at a fair charge. It had no say at all over the levy charged by government to support the now separate range of nuclear power stations.

In the months before stock-exchange flotation, the Board had therefore to decide complex questions about business strategy, bulk-power purchasing and liaison with the Regulator, to say nothing of defending its home territory during the 'open season' before the first annual contracts were settled in July 1990. While the Chairman and Executive Committee handled everything concerning privatisation, Jim Ellis developed two specialist teams, one to buy power, the other to calculate prices, tariffs and to conduct negotiations with larger customers both inside and outside the South East. Both developed highly sophisticated computer models, for Seeboard was entering a market where it could freely choose power from any source available.

During the open season Seeboard won one major contract out of its area, to supply Heathrow Airport, and within, others such as Chessington World of Adventures. But the largest was a £30m double 132 kV line to the Channel Tunnel operator Trans Manche Link to deliver as much energy as the whole Brighton conurbation uses. Out of 180 major users, it lost only nine.

Flotation involved very complex and time-consuming processes, of

Purley Way Superstore, Croydon.

which the 800-page prospectus was only the outward sign. Government, advised by merchant banks and financial experts, did not accept the Board's guarantees unconditionally; but set Touche Ross to make an exhaustive inquest into all twelve. The first draft of their Seeboard report raised problems for the Board since it suggested that although, as a large domestic supplier, Seeboard was freer than most from the economic cycle and should therefore be more attractive to City investors (who were already rating this privatisation highly), staff shortages were inhibiting financial assessment and strategic planning. Seeboard accepted that its financial structure would have to be orientated more commercially than before; but it had legitimate grounds for dissent, since Touche Ross approached it on the same level as all other Boards and undervalued both the work done to cut costs since 1983 and the degree to which management skills and long experience rather than computer number-crunching governed its strategic decisions. Later modified drafts were more acceptable but they still demonstrated how the values and short-term judgements of large investing institutions were to affect Seeboard's conduct in future.

To advise on how best to respond, Seeboard relied heavily on its merchant bankers Morgan Grenfell and its other professional advisers. It became clear that once flotation had occurred, at the set price of 240p per share, on 11 December, the share price would be governed by matters that City analysts could measure: such as information-technology systems, computer analysis, separation of functions, downward pressure on salaries and incentive payments. Morgan Grenfell emphasised that the new shareholders would expect sustained profitability and steady dividend growth, together with flexibility sufficient to cope with the Regulator's requirements. Neither should Seeboard set unrealistic targets in the prospectus, which would only deter the financial institutions.

In the event, such was the success of the advertising campaign mounted in the press and on television to attract small investors, that the offer of 127,381,000 shares was oversubscribed many times. Seeboard staff and pensioners were successfully encouraged to purchase large numbers of shares by allowing them a priority share offer over members of the public. Forty per cent of the successful bids went to small investors, 60 per cent to the financial institutions who had earlier expected to hold at least two-thirds of the total. This should be read as a vindication both of Seeboard's approach to the flotation and consumer loyalty to it in the South East.

□ CHAPTER □
8

Conclusion

Nationalisation opened an era in which memories of the earlier private companies soon faded. Likewise, the newly established Seeboard began to change from its inception; and the next volume of its history will necessarily be very different from this. Yet for the majority of its staff, from linesmen to specialists in offices, shops and training centres, life did not alter at once. The greatest change came naturally on the financial side, as senior managers worked out new long-term business plans, rather than the corporate plans they had earlier drawn up to discuss with the Electricity Council and Ministers. The new Finance Director, John Quin, oversaw a complex process of restructuring which allowed the company to develop an analytical approach that institutional investors in the City now expected. State industry book-keeping, technical rather than strategic, began to give way to computer-based analysis conforming with a range of economic models.

Seeboard owed much to its professional advisers and to the new, slimmed-down management team. Having seen the process through in his last year as Chairman and Chief Executive, George Squair appointed Jim Ellis as Chief Executive and the company announced the appointment of a non-executive Chairman, Sir Keith Stuart, from 1 October 1992. A new generation, trained in business schools, aware that immense opportunities had opened up, staffed the financial-analysis team and demanded information and produced permutations and forecasts of market behaviour. There would be limits of course to innovation, as there had been in the past, but henceforward SEEBOARD plc would be driven by different criteria: by what fund managers wanted to see, and by shareholders' expectations.

Seeboard paid attractive dividends in 1991–2 but, in accordance with its policy of sharing success with shareholders and customers, provided a rebate for domestic and small business customers. This gesture earned OFFER's approbation: Professor Littlechild called it 'welcome and

Sir Keith Stuart, Seeboard Chairman, appointed 1992.

constructive'. But the investment programme also showed that the company sought long-term growth — a safeguard against the temptation to aim for the short-term profits which mattered more to the fund managers.

Within the company, functions were separated into autonomous centres, each responsible for its own budget; the retail sector, reduced after long enquiry to seventy-one shops, was reconstituted as a separate business stream with a 1990–1 turnover of £45m. The engineering sector looked to the challenge of planned replacement. Managing £3 billion worth of assets raises problems as well as economic questions: how to meet public demand for near-perfect security of supply in the maximum safe lifetime of the network without allowing a backlog of renovation to accumulate simply in order to show current profits. The public interest continues to influence all Seeboard's plans.

Jim Ellis, Seeboard Chief Executive, appointed 1992.

Meanwhile the company fought in the market-place to retain its gains, as other regional electricity companies followed its lead to become 'second-tier' operators. Though it gained a number of new large customers, Heathrow reverted to Southern Electric, a loss offset by the huge opportunities opening up at Ashford and West Malling and in the new 'South London Corridor' associated with British Rail's coming high-speed line to Dover and the Channel Tunnel.

One issue which had been dormant since 1948 surfaced again. Seeboard had always been frustrated by the CEGB's monopoly and its refusal to respond to criticisms of the bulk-supply tariff. In March 1988, *Seeboard News* noted 'the generating capacity that will be developed by the Area Boards in their new role must produce pressure to hold down the price'. Discovery of the full costs of decommissioning the older Magnox nuclear plants had forced government to hold on to the nuclear side and to impose a levy on what National Power and PowerGen sold, to keep it profitable under market conditions. Thus the incentive to find alternatives to the new duopoly became overwhelming.

Seeboard could look to Électricité de France with which it had made connection via the National Grid at a special substation in Kent in March 1987 or to the possibility of building its own power station. It asked AES Ltd to begin a study in August 1989 of a small plant, to be fired either by coal or gas, using novel processes which in either case would be environmentally clean.

The great debate about electricity generation and the effects of supply companies' free choice on the future of nuclear energy, the duopoly's policy towards imported coal and the effects on British coal mines, took place on a different level. Seeboard had a duty to its customers to buy in the cheapest secure market, within OFFER's rules, and hence required source diversity as well as a low *current* price, whatever the

Facing page: The helicopter today is a basic item of maintenance equipment. Here Seeboard engineer Roy Plummer (left) conducts a routine check of overhead electricity lines at Fulking in West Sussex. He and his colleagues regularly check 13,000 km of overhead lines.

structure government had created in 1988–90, and whatever individuals felt about the choices involved. (There had been only sporadic protests about nuclear development in the South East and, until the true cost of nuclear power was revealed, Seeboard had no reason to doubt Department of Energy and CEGB figures; and had supported these claims by visiting the two Dungeness stations in 1986.)

It was and is the Regulator's unenviable task to try to ensure greater diversity, despite the duopoly, and to prevent National Power and PowerGen, with their remarkably similar pricing policies, from manipulating prices in the pooling system – about which the Major Energy Users Council soon complained – initially by supporting the regional electricity companies' search for alternatives. So Seeboard went ahead with the Medway gas-fired power station recommended by AES Ltd to supply up to 660 MW; and negotiated with Électricité de France for up to 100 MW more, energy at 0.3p less than the pool's average.

Beyond this, Seeboard has become a total energy company, by buying gas from the North Sea and selling it via British Gas pipelines to smaller industrial and commercial customers cheaper (because of its lower margin and local orientation) than can British Gas. On the way to becoming the leading supplier of energy in the South East, it has no fear that British Gas would be able to do the same with electricity.

Market forces operate in two ways in the supply industry. Apart from buying energy economically, Seeboard has to deliver it safely and securely, as well as cheaply. The free choice open to large industrial customers acts as one discipline, the Regulator the other. Professor Littlechild can compel a company to make refunds to small customers if he suspects overcharging or not buying cheaply enough (which is also a constraint on the long-term choice between gas and coal). There remains a commercial risk that, if cost alone rules, safety and security of supply may suffer. It is noticeable that Seeboard has sought carefully to co-operate with OFFER and the licence conditions and to provide only verifiable statistics of performance, not vague claims – not least because of what shareholders expect. Beyond that forum, the privatised company is also subject to media and parliamentary enquiry to a much greater extent than it was as a state industry, whose Ministers had no statutory obligation to reply to detailed questions.

Self-regulation, well understood in the City, is the key: backed up by the Regulator. And self-regulation is easier for a company in competition with others than if it were part of a privatised monopoly. Staff also benefit from greater managerial freedom. Senior Managers now have individual contracts, staff generally have more flexible hours and in some cases the chances to work from home, using hand-held terminals programmed by telephone line (modem) each Sunday night for the following week. Bonus payments have become possible; out-of-hours work is now done centrally by a team integrating field-workers and head office twenty-four hours a day.

The freedom to manage and to shape the firm's identity may have a price: regional electricity companies will find it hard to replicate the Electricity Council's research facility into the high technology of supply – something which the French government still provides for Électricité de France. Co-operation between former Boards, in their wider interest, may permit this; depending on whether they all retain what was most important from the nationalised period. The old Seeboard adopted a resolution at its final meeting in February 1990, that it should take pride in the past and should ensure continuity with the future. Forty-two years as a state industry had bequeathed 'a tradition of excellence in meeting the needs of its customers', which would be 'carried forward into the next century'.

Seeboard stands at the interface of technology and public: it will always be a utility. It has to innovate to survive, yet it must also be conservative enough not to take risks which might interrupt supply or make it unsafe. There are no short cuts in any modern country. Its business is to give power to customers in both senses of the word. State-run industries tended always to prescribe for consumers towards whom their duty was essentially paternalistic. As a PLC, Seeboard deals with customers who have high expectations, who have access to the facts, and who are aware of their rights in ways which only major users enjoyed in the past. As a Seeboard community newspaper *Seeboard Links* put it, in the autumn 1991 issue: 'We are a company in the community and have a commitment to help.'

Appendix I

Senior Executives

CHAIRMEN

Sir Norman Elliott	1948–62
W. R. T. Skinner	1962–63
H. V. Pugh CBE	1963–66
E. Sinnott OBE	1966–74
A. G. Milne	1974–75
T. Rutherford CBE	1975–77
R. A. Peddie	1977–83
G. A. Squair	1983–92
Sir Keith Stuart	1992–

DEPUTY CHAIRMEN

W. R. T. Skinner	1948–62
E. Sinnott OBE	1962–66
A. G. Milne	1966–74
J. A. Wedgwood CBE	1974–77
L. W. Goacher	1977–82
A. W. Nicol	1982–87
D. A. Lovesey	1987–91
(Managing Director 1990)	
T. J. Ellis	1992–
(Chief Executive)	

CHIEF OFFICERS

Engineer

W. A. Gallon	1948–52
W. E. Gibbs	1952–65
E. Peel	1965–78
W. Kerss	1978–84
L. Jones OBE	1984–
(Operations Director)	

Accountant

E. Sinnott OBE	1948–62
A. Dent	1962–70
F. W. Shaw	1970–74
L. W. Goacher	1974–77
F. W. Barnes	1977–81
P. F. Humpherson	1982–89
(Finance Director)	
J. B. Quin	1989–
(Finance Director)	

Commercial Manager

C. F. Wells	1948–55
E. H. Skinner	1955–65
I. M. MacKay	1965–70
L. J. Simmons	1970–76
R. E. Gleadow	1976–78
D. J. Fuller	1978–86
T. J. Ellis	1986–91
(Commercial Director)	

Secretary

A. L. Burnell	1948–58
G. Wray OBE	1958–72
D. A. Green	1972–80
P. F. Humpherson	1980–81
S. M. Wide	1981–93
(also Administration Director)	

Corporate Strategy Director

T. A. Boley	1990–93

Appendix II

Consumers, Unit Sales and Staff Numbers:
1949–1987

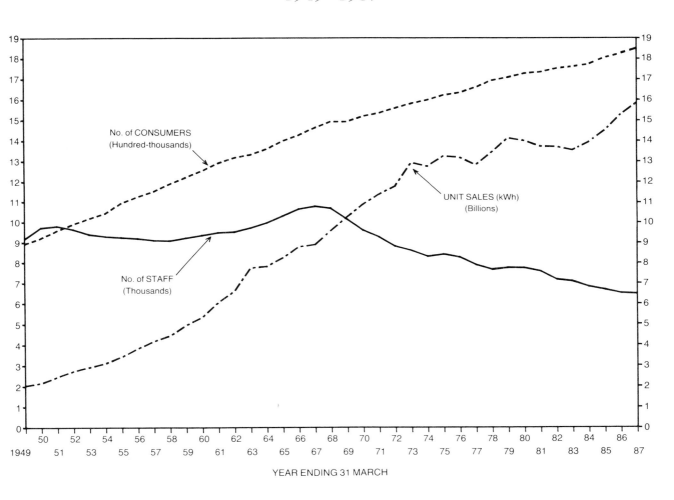

YEAR ENDING 31 MARCH

Appendix III

Comparative Performance Figures 1985 – 1986*

	Seeboard	Average all Boards
Net return on average net assets (%)	3.30	3.10
Added operating costs per customer (£)	68.80	77.50
Distribution costs per customer (£)	40.39	47.89
Adminstration costs per customer (£)	10.04	10.69
Meter reading bill and collection cost per customer (£)	5.81	7.07
Employees per 1000 customers	2.86	3.19
Average minutes per customer lost due to faults	62.80	66.80
Sales to industry (%)	24.20	—
Number of customers per square mile (1987–8)	233	—

*Taken from Area Board Review, Section C of Performance Indicators 1987–8 (Electricity Council).

Index

(Figures in italics refer to illustrations)